# The Power

# of

# No Thought

## A Direct Approach to Self-Discovery

M. J. Mossafa

Translation by Saeed Emdadi

Rumi Rapture Series

Rumi Rapture Series
1429 Kew Gardens Ct.
San Jose, CA 95120

www.rumirapture.com


The Power of No Thought/ M.J.Mossafa, Saeed Emdadi

1st edition

Printed in the United States of America

ISBN: 978-0615931388

# Table of Contents

# PREFACE

H ave you wondered why the human race has histori-
cally been subjected to living in a state of conflict,
fear, and confusion? Is an uninterrupted, continuous state of
happiness possible? If yes, how does one get it? Why are nearly
all human beings suffering even after hundreds of years of written and spoken words about salvation? What obstacles prevent
nearly all of us from attaining inner freedom? Have the very few
actually been successful in cracking the code? Can the self-
liberating process be experienced by anyone?

Mr. M. J. Mossafa takes a novel approach in the self-
discovery of our unconscious mental habits, from childhood on-
ward, that lead to building a false sense of identity. Through a
simple system of dissecting thought processes and question-and-
answer discussions, Mossafa masterfully explains, in simple
words, how to eliminate our habituated stumbling blocks and
consciously replace them with an "unlearning process" that will
point the reader to his/her authentic and natural state of self.

**-Translator**

# FOREWORD

I t might be of interest to remember the circumstances that made this book available to you. If you have read it cover to cover, more than once, and your thirst for the truth has not diminished but rather increased, take it as a road sign for being on the path. If you discarded it as something nonsensical or what you knew already, consider that you may be reacting to something. Some believe that we will all get on the path eventually. It is evident that physical death is the end of all physical existence for the body, the mind, the feelings, and the thoughts. However, is it also the end of our awareness? Awareness is not thought, it is not the weak voice in your head telling you to give up thoughts; that is nothing but another cunning thought. Awareness is spirituality, it has no voice, it has nothing, and it is no-thought. Don't be fooled otherwise. Awareness is not physical and it does not die at death.

This work, created in Persian by Mr. Mossafa, was first published in Iran in 1985. The author is one of the rare individuals with an in-depth understanding of the genuine Sufi teachings, who toiled many years in the study of the mind. His experience enabled him to delve into the depths of a particular group of

Rumi's verses in the Masnavi,[1] rarely found in any other published works of the grand sage, and elucidate their hidden meaning. This book and the future ones in the Rumi Rapture series make few references to Rumi as a person and his life. Such references can be found elsewhere and familiarity with Rumi might be inspiring for readers. Here, however, the common aim of the author and the translator is to depict the highest and the most intricate levels of Rumi's self-awareness teachings. The focus in this book has been on important messages that Rumi set out to convey through his words to people of all backgrounds, creeds, races, and religions over the centuries following his death.

*"My name and my words will be told among the lovers, centuries after my death."*
     -Rumi

That which Rumi truly meant by Love, Life, Existence, Happiness, Rapture, Time, and Now can be understood intellectually, emotionally, and spiritually at many levels. The timeless message of Rumi and his care for mankind transcend cultures and beliefs. He was a non-denominational teacher, who at all times provides the guiding light for humanity to find the only purpose of life, and emphasizes the gift of the discovery of our true nature.

---

[1] The Masnavi is a masterpiece of Mawlana Jalaluddin Rumi, who lived in the 13th century. The Masnavi consists mainly of Sufi teachings through stories with profound mystical and psychological interpretations. The Masnavi is a series of six books of poetry that amount to nearly 26,000 verses.

Rumi has created many works, some in large volumes. Many translations of his works into English have been produced over the past centuries, each with a particular focus toward an aspect of his works. There are poetry translations by renowned writers that convey his language of Love eloquently. Then there are philosophical writings, storytelling, ethics and religious teachings that are recited by millions of people in many languages. There are also songs and chants of Rumi's poetry and worship that serve as the fuel of enchantment for gatherings practiced in the Living Nights.

This book is different, however, in that it focuses on self-realization and the psychological aspects of Rumi's works. Unlike Modern Psychology, it is less concerned with behaviorism. It strives to reach the depths of the human psyche by examining the source of thoughts and the false need for the formation of human individuality and separation from the rest of existence. Here the author explores the physical and spiritual forces operating within us as humans, with special focus on what goes on inside the human mind that both connects us to the Absolute and at the same time prevents that connection.

Another focus of the book is on the experience of not-being, while illustrating how to seek out, find, and eliminate that which drives us incessantly yet is not our true nature. On this quest, that which we are is made clear. This process works reversely to what our logical expectations might demand. That is, we find what we are by peeling away the layers encasing us in a colossal, make-believe game to cover and misrepresent what we are.

The author spent years of painstaking studies and self-discovery practices to acquire knowledge from Eastern and

Western sources to crack the code on the how-to methods of self-discovery, self-realization, going-within, *satori (state of consciousness),* or any other applicable name given to the process of spiritual domination over the self. He later came across a category of Rumi's writings that had shown the principles of the task at hand, the definition of the problem, the pitfalls along the way, and above all the questioning of the person in charge of our deceptions, which is none other than us.

It is truly remarkable to see Rumi, an educator in several disciplines some eight hundred years ago, with hundreds of students and family responsibilities, had dedicated the time to discover the most intricate workings of the human mind, bringing them into practice and writing about them for future generations.

Mr. Mossafa, a practicing ascetic, has received many seekers in organized lectures, followed by discussions in private settings, offering his knowledge and experience of the innermost Sufi teachings. With little reference to religious doctrines, he takes students through the rockiest realms of self-knowledge, from the obligations inherent in our human lives, to the highest reaches of the secret of secrets, the Absolute Truth.

To this end, the readers must be mindful that the presented texts are excerpts from his lectures, in which he presents these truths and repeatedly reviews them until the student receives a deep appreciation for the materials. Not unlike many teachers of the path, the author is direct in his approach of the nurturing of his students. The initiate who is confronted by the ego may not receive this style without a fight. However, an adept learner knows that there is little time and much to accomplish.

**-Translator**

Calligraphy by Koorosh Azadi: Rumi's introduction of Masnavi
"Listen to the reed how it tells a tale, complaining of separations."

# CHAPTER ONE

# WHO TAUGHT YOU HOW TO THINK?

F rom an early age, the human mind becomes accustomed to viewing life circumstances from two distinct perspectives and relates to them each in a certain way: one is an objective perspective and the other interpretive.

For instance, I might notice you are walking in a peculiar way, moving your arms rapidly, taking long strides or hunched over, and I may attach to this no particular interpretation or meaning. However, if I am not satisfied with this perspective, I might analyze it from a different viewpoint and see something else. I might interpret the way you walk as having a particular meaning, and that interpretation may be far from the reality. This interpretation is the result of a mental or moral judgment. For example, I might interpret the way you walk as undignified, proud, or pitiful. We relate to all life's circumstances and phenomena in a similar manner.

We may look at a couch from two perspectives: one as a means of restful seating and the other as a means of distinction and pride of possession.

# THE POWER OF NO THOUGHT

We might be hungry and hope that our often-visited restaurant has prepared our favorite dish, but unfortunately, upon arriving at the restaurant we find that it's not on the menu. Not seeing the desired item on the menu and feeling hungry are real; however, we might view this affair from a totally different perspective that is not related to the reality of the situation. Perhaps we might think that the restaurant owner does not consider us an important patron or other kinds of interpretations. This is simply our mind's interpretation of the reality.

The mental perspective or "interpretive" viewpoint in human beings is neither natural nor necessary. This habitual mental activity is often redundant or superfluous. As we shall point out later, this imposition of the interpretive aspect of the mind causes a lot of problems that result in human suffering.

In these discussions, we shall explore how these destructive suggestions get impressed upon the human mind, what characteristics they embody, and how they become the cause of needless preoccupation and suffering. We shall then address how we can prevent the mind from this kind of unnecessary and destructive activity.

In order to clearly understand such problems, it is important to look at our interpersonal relationships with each other, especially the quality of our relationships with children, without confusing ourselves with hypotheses and generalities. The relationship we have with our children is mostly the same as the relationship our elders had with us when we were children, due to similar upbringings and conditions. If we pay attention to the ways in which we behave toward our children, we can understand our problems in a tangible and accurate manner as beginning in our childhood and continuing to present.

Suppose a number of children are playing in a park and get into a dispute with each other, and we witness one of the kids hitting another. Since our minds are *trained to interpret* all behaviors and events, we might think of the kid who hit the other, as a "brave kid" or a "wild kid." In regards to the child who has been hit, we might think, "what a timid and incapable kid."

On a parallel theme, when we see a child sharing his toys or edibles with another child, we might think "what a generous kid" or we might think "what a dumb kid" that gives away his belongings to others for no reason. We certainly are familiar with such interpretations. Every day we interpret our own and others' behaviors, tens of times in different manners, explicitly or implicitly, by words, by behaviors, by our looks or bodily gestures, or by our silence.

Now let's see, step by step, what the results of these interpretations are after we as children unknowingly become conditioned by certain perspectives—what interactions might take place in our minds, and what perceptions we might derive from life and relationships.

Certainly, the first assumption we make as children is that any movement, behavior, or circumstance in human relationship has an attached specific meaning like an invisible shadow. We understand that hitting or getting hit by another is not merely an action but carries a hidden meaning as well. Sharing food with another kid is a reality, but it also means "generosity." Thus, from an early age the child's mind learns an "interpretive" quality in relation to life. As a result, we become accustomed to perceiving an experience not in its true reality, but rather in looking for a meaning and a label after any action or experience.

It would seem to a child that an action without an interpretation is incomplete. As though, interpretation and labeling are inseparable from objects and circumstances. Later in life, the human mind learns to replace true understanding of circumstances with its interpretations, gradually making it difficult to free oneself from the chains of mental captivity. Realities and their interpretations become ingrained in our minds as one and the same, inseparable from one another. That is why human beings most often cannot see the realities of life as they are. In each person's view, every reality should also have an explanation and an interpretation, even though the explanation and the interpretation are merely mental habits. Moreover, the habit from childhood of mixing interpretation and reality together into one unit would make them indistinguishable and inseparable in adulthood.

Gradually, as we grow and expand our familiarity with interpretations ever so unconsciously, we also begin to notice that all interpretations, although made up of different words, topics, and justifications, center on one thing: "value." The forms of interpretation may be varied, but there is a hidden message behind all of them and that is value. As we become familiar with life, we also learn that the goal of life and relationships is to attract "value" and avoid anything "valueless."

Another logical assumption we make as children is derived from the way people conduct their lives and the quality of their relationships, in that the interpretation of realities as valuable or valueless is more important than the actual realities themselves. When a kid is hit and suffers physical pain, we do not pay much attention to his or her pain. What becomes more important than their pain is our interpretation of he/she getting hit. The kid understands very well from our behaviors that the expression "coward" is more important for us than the pain he/she suffers. In a similar manner, the essence of sharing food with another child is less important to us than the value ascribed to "generosity."

If we pay closer attention to our current situation, we can see that our mental interpretation of circumstances is more important than the actual reality. If, more than twenty years ago, somebody slapped us or deprived us of food and we went hungry for a day, the physical pain of getting slapped or the denial of food may easily have been forgotten as insignificant. However, the pain of "what a weak and cowardly person I am" is still registered in our memories and continues to haunt us. The feeling of hunger that we had on that day as a reality does not bother us any longer as much as the notion mentioned on the previous page: "the restaurant owner did not consider us an important patron." This notion is still with us and continues to bother us.

Since we give more importance to interpretive values than we do realities, this causes two fundamental problems tragic in their nature.

The first problem pertains to human relationships with the outside world. Once the human mind is engrossed with values as vital necessities, it becomes so infatuated and preoccupied with those values that it is no longer aware of the real world and its happenings. As a result, we create a new existence and a special world from all those superficial and extraneous values, and we end up living in that "self-created" world. The values mesmerize the human mind in the true sense of the word, attracting and imprisoning us and blinding our attention to the world's realities.

As a result, instead of relating to life, we establish a relationship with the shadow of life. As it is said, we live in a dream. That is, we become separated from reality and create a world from illusion, thought, images, and interpretations, and that is the world we live in.

The second problem is the disconnection that happens between ourselves and our essence. In the process of getting acquainted with values, the natural characteristics of our human essence become veiled or covered and instead we become ruled by social norms. As children, some innate states and qualities still exist that guide our actions and behaviors. For instance, based on some innate quality, we may or may not desire to share our food with others. Based on the dictation of our nature, we become social or antisocial. By our nature, we may be calm and forgiving or difficult to deal with. These and many other characteristics and qualities that arise from our natural states make up our human essence and guide our lives. That is, until we get acquainted with interpretive language.

As children, we do not tell ourselves, "Since I'm social I should socialize with others"; or "since I'm generous I should share my food with others." Rather, our human nature dictates how to behave. However, after acquaintance with interpretive values, our relationship with our inner state declines and we act according to what is dictated by values. After the word "generous" is registered in our minds as a valuable quality that everyone should have, we no longer pay attention to our inner inclinations; we always feel obliged to act "generous."

After the mind is dominated by values, we no longer care to listen to our inner voice. We alienate our own nature, and we lose our relationship to our inner states. Then, our behavior, our relationships, and our lives are ruled by external phenomena weighing on our minds. In other words, a "natural human" is transformed into a "conventional human." *(Please be aware that we are moving forward into the investigation of these problems, step by step.)*

In parallel with these circumstances, another problem arises. From all of the accumulated interpretations of the human mind, an elusive existence arises that we accept as the "I" or as mental identity. Before getting acquainted with the language of interpretation, we had yet to conceive of any such experience of ourselves as an "I." We have inner qualities, but we have not yet formed an "I" from those qualities, because we have not attached any labels to ourselves such as "I am brave, humble, generous, smart, incapable," etc.

However, as soon as other human beings interpret a child's qualities and behaviors with either a value or a valueless attribute—meaning, we identify those qualities for the child by characterizations and labels—then they get registered in the child's mind and an elusive mental center is created. This elusive mental center will be taken by the child as the "I," or his mental identity. *(In the next chapter, we shall have a detailed discussion about the "I" and its characteristics. This brief mention is sufficient for now.)*

Interpretive values have expanding and spreading behaviors

like malignant tumors. Once this pattern is imprinted in the mind, it forms a center of corruption whose dimensions will increase day after day. Each attribute bears other attributes and problems, which in turn, multiply as well.

One of the attributes of interpretive values is the mind's "comparative" outlook. Every interpretive value can only be conceived by comparing it with its opposite (and both sides exist due to the mind's embellishments, not due to their own independent existences.) For instance, if you do not compare "capable" with "incapable," neither one will make sense. If you do not have any perception about "stinginess," "generosity" does not mean anything to you. Being "shy" is only conceivable when set opposite to being "social," and "inferiority" in comparison to "superiority," etc. All superficial and conventional values have such a quality.

In contrast, real phenomena, as opposed to interpretive values, are independent of opposites. Cold is a real quality that can be sensed without comparing it to warm. Interestingly, our minds sense the real qualities of each experience by means of comparing them against each other too, due to the developed *habit of comparison*. Thus, such comparisons further add to human sufferings. If we do not compare the hot summer with the cool spring weather, the hot summer is not necessarily aggravating.

Let's examine what kind of problems will arise from the "comparative" attribute of values. Comparison breeds competition. If it is not for competition, what is it that pushes us in every step of life to compare ourselves with others? Doesn't the continuous comparison indicate that we are engaged in hidden struggle and competition with each other? Take a close look at your relationships, and see whether this is not the case!

For instance, when I say that my child has learned to count from one to one hundred, you may immediately say that your child has learned to swim. Perhaps I read some poetry from Rumi and wanted to show off my knowledge of his works. In response, you may immediately brag about your knowledge of Hafiz. If we watch closely, we can see there are a series of comparisons and a sense of underlying competition. And of course comparison and competition are not always direct; rather they are often covered with justifications.

If we honestly examine the roots of our sufferings and problems, we find that, except for physical pains, there is no pain or hardship that is not born out of comparison and competition.

Obviously, children grow in the same environment as the rest of us and clearly see the truth of their circumstances. They see, for instance, that the way their parents conduct themselves at home or at work, the way they dress, eat, respect or disrespect each other, their manners, etc., is different from what they display when they are with others outside the home or in the workplace. From these dual behaviors and shows of pretense, the child develops a logical perception that there is a subtle, mysterious, and unadvertised war going on among human beings. All the values and principles covered under the umbrella of "upbringing"—as presented to and imposed upon the child—are in fact tools and weapons for the same war.

Thus, this process causes us one of the most fundamental and destructive changes in human life. Our interest and attention become divested from the truth of life, and we only think about competitive advantages. We believe and behave as though we are in a combat zone, and our goal is to furnish ourselves with more tools and weapons for this war. Therefore, we look at life experiences only as the means and weaponry of war. This approach to life automatically sets us up in a negative direction; and we are forced into the battlefield. Who knows the degree of gravity hidden in this change of course! After exposure to values as weapons of combat, humans lose their sense of life. In other words, we do not live truly or live freely, but devote our lives and existences to fighting off a myriad of empty and rhetorical values.

By analogy, it is like I am standing in a vast open field, but I am told to look in one direction only. When I look at life from a competitive perspective, the goal and the meaning of life are then defined by the fight and struggle for that competitive advantage. It is true that I will follow different goals, different activities. I might write a book, gain wealth, chase fame and status etc., but I will only view all of that from one perspective. I will see everything within the framework of gaining advantage and domination in the hidden fight and struggle for values. Is there not a huge loss in this process? Is it not a tragedy to lose the breadth of life and see only one dimension? Does life have only one goal and one meaning? Isn't this a dreadful, corrosive, and corrupt dimension in which to live?!

We said that an elusive center gets created in the mind of a child due to the collection of values that result in the false "I." Also, we said that one of the basic attributes of such values is its "comparative" quality. Now let's see what further problems are caused by this process.

# WHO TAUGHT YOU HOW TO THINK?

It is obvious that when it comes to comparisons, no one can absolutely claim that their personal attributes are "the most valuable." There is always someone whose value exceeds our own. For example, one day Peter wins the wrestling match against David, or he is able to sing the school anthem better than David does. We tell Peter, "Well done! What a capable and smart kid." This is a common process we are all familiar with. By doing this, we have hung the invisible medal for "being the most valuable" around Peter's neck and raised him on the honor platform.

On another day, instead of David, Michael wrestles with Peter, and he is able to knock Peter out or sing the school anthem better than he does. We appropriately rescind the values that we offered to Peter on that day and give them to Michael. Tomorrow, such medals may move from Michael to John or someone else. So is the process by which a human being lives throughout his entire life.

Values are presented to and infused in children such that it seems to them that they are the dearest things that anyone could have. At the same time children have also begun to form a solid mental center as the "I" or "identity" that they recognize as their psychological existence. However, due to their comparative make up, these values are impermanent and unreliable. In other words, we have established our psychological structures and identities over something that changes every moment. In view of these influences, are we not constantly in fear, anxiety, despair, lack of trust, and a deep feeling of insecurity? (I hope the friends who read books with titles such as "How to Empower Self-Confidence" or those who say, "Happy are those who have self-confidence," pay attention to these principles: Which self do you have "confidence" in? Which self can you trust when the foundation of your identity is based on a bunch of interpretive and empty values? How can you trust in a phenomenon that is nothing but shadow and imagery? *Can* such "confidence" or "identity" be trusted?

In the process of comparing, we are continually granted certain values, and then they are inevitably taken away from us. Since values form our existence and psychological identities, any time a value is taken away from us, we feel as if a piece of our existence has been carved out and a part of our psychological life harmed. When this happens, what kind of feeling or impression do we have toward others and ourselves? We end up having the notion that we need to be cleverer, more capable, and more knowledgeable than the person with whom we are comparing ourselves. These qualities seem necessary and vital, yet when we compare ourselves to others, we inevitably find ourselves lacking and feel that something essential is somehow missing in us. In this case, wouldn't we carry a feeling of inferiority, deficiency, and worthlessness?

Why do you think we are never satisfied with our current situation? Why do we often live with regret—regret due to something that we think we should have had but we don't. Why is it that wherever we get to, we continue to run with more thirst and greed to get to somewhere else? Why do we always look to the future? Doesn't living in the future indicate that we see deficiency in our current situation that we need to compensate for in the future? If we pay close attention, we see that this process makes up our everyday lives, that is, when we wake up in the morning we are faced with thoughts such as, "I have an incomplete and undesirable character and I should change it to something other than what it is." Repeatedly, this process prevails throughout our lives.

Under such conditions, can we have desirable feelings towards each other? Each one of us is an agent of intimidation for the other, and hence we feel threatened by each other. As long as human relations are dominated by comparison and competition, any hope of true kindness and love is impossible. For as long as competition exists, inferiority and fear will also exist. These two are obstructive to love and any kind of desirable feeling.

If we believe our value exceeds the value of others, the result is a sort of intoxicating feeling, which is simultaneously accompanied by fear and anxiety. This is due to our perception that this value can be taken away. Today you are a boss but tomorrow you may not be. If, in our minds, the value or worth of others exceed ours, the result would be a feeling of inferiority, unhappiness, regret, and hatred. What is missing in the comparative and competitive relationship is the lack of the feeling of equality.

Our relationships are determined by values. We know that interpretive values are not limited to just one or two. There are hundreds of different values that make up our identity. With respect to some of these values we have the feeling of superiority, and with respect to some others we lack the same feeling. Therefore, our relationship with each other is dualistic and contradictory. This is a combination of feeling our self-importance and our inferiority. (Of course, due to some reasons that we shall explain later, we tend to have more feelings of inferiority than self-importance. In fact, our feelings of self-importance are just a cover to disguise our feelings of inferiority.)

We have all experienced a sense of worry and hesitation when meeting someone. This is because it is not clear how we should approach a new person. In the first few moments, we might start assessing the other's value or worth. If we find that value superior to ours, we take a subordinate attitude and behavior, and if they are the opposite, we adjust our behavior with a sense of superiority. When we meet someone for the first time, the first question we ask is his or her profession. By means of determining that profession, we would adjust our approach in relating to that person.

The interpretive relationship implicitly indicates another principle, which translates into not being in touch with others' human essence. I have no business with your human essence; it's your face value that's important to me. Because from the time I was born, my preoccupation has been with value not with essence. Hence our relationship is the relationship of value with value and not the relationship of human with human. In other words, such relationship is the relationship of two objects or two images, not the relationship of two humans, each with his or her essence and nature. In reality, when I come to visit you, I meet your face identity, meaning that I've come to visit the phenomenon that is labeled "boss." In my mind, you are the owner of high status, which is stuck on you like an invisible label.

This relationship is not a real relationship, but a situation that is fraught with potential evasion, escape, and defense. Our values act as a shield, a defensive quality that we use to hide ourselves behind. Have you noticed how you use your personality

14

as a way to guard yourself from another? How cautiously you make yourself known to others and not allow them to easily get close to your world of values.

Another problem created by competitive and comparative relationships is that it automatically draws us toward a shallow, superficial, and pretentious life. Once we get caught in a fighting mode, we look at everything as a target of competition and automatically lose interest in the essence of experience and its realities. We not only look at life one dimensionally, but we also fail to look at that one dimension methodically. Our interest and our attention increase only as a means of getting ahead of our known and unknown rivals.

Suppose a person is learning a foreign language. If they have genuine interest in the language itself, their learning will have a deep and profound quality. But if they are learning the language to show off that they also know a foreign language, they will learn only as far as that intention is fulfilled. Their situation is like a soldier who tries to fake that his gun is loaded and ready to fire. It's not important that his weapon is empty. It is only important that the enemy gets the impression that his weapon is loaded and ready to fire.

\*\*\*

This is not a discussion about a hypothetical subject or a hypothetical human being. It is about our current situation. Therefore, we need to search and perhaps recognize that the problems and specifics I am pointing to currently exist in all of us. The competitive perspectives imposed upon us from early childhood are now dominating all our relationships.

The problems and their characteristics derived from the interpretive perspective in all our relationships are broad and far-reaching and not limited to the ones I have mentioned here. Many other problems and complications in all areas of our lives arise from our interpretative values and our pretentious conduct. When we speak of human beings as being out of touch with reality and living in a world of "self-made" values, this condition permeates every aspect of life. We emphasize, pay attention to, and think more about the face value of our job than the actual work we are doing. The face value that we give to our furniture and our cars preoccupies our minds such that we do not even notice the reality of the furniture and the car. In married life, the face value of having a spouse has become more important than the person we are married to. If unmarried, in some cases, the feeling of worthlessness for not having a spouse causes more distress than the reality of being single. The type of spouse that we choose is often influenced more by face value than the real qualities of the person. In general, we are dominated by the concept of value rather than reality.

At the end of each chapter I will try to clarify the subjects discussed through questions and answers that arose in my sessions with others.

\*\*\*

**Q:** *What is the cause of this interpretive perspective in the way that we relate with each other as human beings? You say that this type of perspective is unnatural and superfluous. How-*

*ever, since it is here, we could say that it is a natural and an unavoidable necessity.*

**A:** What do you mean by "natural"? We know that breathing, eating, sleeping, talking, etc., is instinctive or natural. These properties have always existed in human beings, but is this true of the interpretive perspective?

**Q:** *If it is not natural, why is it in us?*

**A:** Knowing why, how, and when it was created is not useful to us. The reality is that the language of interpretation already exists and it causes us pain and suffering. Therefore, the problem that we need to deal with is whether we can free ourselves from the divisiveness of interpretive viewpoints.

We carry a heavy load on our shoulders. Who, when, and why this heavy load was put on our shoulders is not of importance. The more important concern is how to unload this heavy burden so that we can walk and live freely. My point is that a bunch of face values that are not even shadows of reality, get imposed on our minds, and they have created hundreds of serious problems for us. Now the question is how can we expel these superfluous mental burdens from our minds so that we can liberate ourselves and live peacefully?

**Q:** *Do you consider all notions of social value to be mental? In my opinion there is a need for some values in society, and that authentic human values should be fostered.*

**A:** It seems like the difference between the two types of perspective and relationships we are talking about is still not clear to you. Let me try to clarify.

Let's assume that a child has a fear of the dark. The fear is an undesirable feeling. I'm not saying that this condition is solely mental. The child's fear is a reality. What I'm saying is that if we look at this presumably undesirable reality simply as reality and nothing else, meaning that we do not complicate matters by condemning it as valueless, then it would simply have an undesirable quality. At that point, the problem is only one. But when we say "what a timid child," the problem becomes two: one is the undesirable reality of fear, the other is the valueless impression that the child ascribes to him or herself. It's the second problem, the interpretive aspect that causes pain, trouble and conflict between human beings. I do not deny that there are desirable or undesirable realities. The only point that I'm making is that when we interpret desirable and undesirable as valuable and valueless, the problem shows another side.

Hunger is an undesirable reality, but if we look at hunger as a valueless quality, then this negative interpretation of hunger becomes more important than the actual feeling of hunger. Then, instead of trying to satisfy hunger, our attention is on grieving its worthless quality. The impression of "what a deprived and poor human being I am" becomes a lot more painful than the actual feeling of being hungry. The mind's preoccupation with the impression of "poor and helpless" hinders finding a proper and logical solution to hunger.

**Q:** *Does not life become arid and dead if we only look at and relate to realities?*

**A:** This subject is very simple and we do not need to make it complex. Let's say a young boy has certain innate qualities and dispositions, and he does things accordingly. For example, he may or may not like to share his food with another child. Now, whether or not we appreciate his generosity, the innate quality upon which he bases his act does not disappear. That desire is part of his human nature and it stays with him through any act of generosity in the future. But after we praise his generosity, his subsequent generous actions will be associated with words of praise and not based on his inner call. This means that a bunch of words and expressions become a director of his behavior and his life rather than his natural desire. So, in what sense would you be saying that life becomes arid and dead? In the absence of interpretations, life is more meaningful, richer, and far superior in spirit than the current situation we live in. In fact, his present situation is arid due to his drifting away from his innate qualities.

**Q:** *Isn't competition necessary for progress?*

**A:** Are you referring to spiritual and moral progress or progress in materialistic affairs?

**Q:** *Progress in both.*

**A:** In the context of morality and spirituality, neither the reality nor the reason indicates that competition leads to progress. In truth, if competition were the cause of progress in morality, given all the existing competitions in the world, human beings would have gone beyond the heavens by now. They would not be struggling in this moralistic hell. Logically, competition is not a valid motive for the progress of morality nor of spirituality. In fact, what does competition mean in the context of spirituality? What does this concept really mean? Suppose you are a brave, charming, kind, and humble person. These attributes form your spirituality. Let's say I want to compete with you in the context of those attributes and get ahead of you, and let's be optimistic and assume that the talent for such attributes potentially and naturally exists in me as well. Now you tell me what should I do to let these attributes grow in me and become even better than yours?

If attributes such as courage, kindness, and humility are naturally part of my inner substance, whether I want them to be or not, they would automatically thrive. Their growth is beyond my will and consciousness, and so there are no real obstacles to prevent their growth. And if these attributes do not exist in me naturally, there would be nothing for me to try to make better than yours. In principle, true spiritual qualities cannot be quantified, and therefore we cannot wish to have more or less of them. Love, kindness, courage, and humility are ineffable. We do not know their essence and quality. Hence, how can I compete with an unknown quality?

However, from one perspective your comment about the necessity of competition is correct. Since we mistake the pretension of spiritual attributes for spirituality, it is possible to imagine such a progress. My *pretense* of generosity, courage, humility, or any other attributes may be better than yours. Currently, spirituality in nearly any society is nothing but these pretensions.

Competition in worldly matters does not cause progress. Soon we will explain that hundreds of obstacles are created and caused by a competitive relationship, which in turn block or waste our natural talents. For example, pretentious living, all kinds of conflicts, escape from realities, and excursion into the realm of self-created and elusive worlds, all kinds of fears, and many other problems cause human stagnation and lack of movement. If these inner obstacles do not exist, perhaps human beings would have gotten what you consider to be symbols of progress thousands of years earlier. Such progress would have a constructive quality, rather than the destructive quality it has now. Regardless, there is still this question that in spite of all advancements that have been the result of competition, have human beings actually become fortunate?

**Q:** *But if there is no competition, human beings would not have any motive to progress.*

**A:** In the case of present human beings, yes, it is like that. Competition, and the anger and hatred derived from it, are like fuel to the motor of our individual personalities and lives. But if those same human beings were to honestly resign from competition, they could reach their human essence, and this would be the quality that stimulated their progress, without need for thoughts and perceptions of progress or regress.

# CHAPTER TWO

# HOW THE "I" GETS CREATED

In the previous chapter, I stated that within societies certain interpretive values become attached to reality like invisible shadows. They have no real existence in the essence of our experiences. However, when these interpretive values are registered in the mind, a "center" is developed that we then consider to be the "I" or self-identity. Thereafter, this artificial mental center becomes the source of some dramatic changes, a few of which were explained in the previous chapter. Now, let's expand our understanding of this mental phenomenon by exploring some of its less obvious drawbacks.

First, let's consider what the human attributes are at birth. Then we will see whether the thing we perceive as the "I," also known as "personality," is what we were born with or whether it has migrated from its original reality and become something different.

As human beings we are born with certain physical and mental qualities that collectively make up our basic nature, meaning a collection of attributes that separate us from other living beings. For instance, we may at times display expressions

23

of passion or joy, fear, anxiety, or anger, and for some unknown reason we may not like certain things. Sometimes we are rough and at other times gentle. Sometimes we like to have a relationship with others, and at other times, we like to be by ourselves. We have certain needs and many other qualities as part of our human nature.

Presently, we have accumulated certain mental ideas about ourselves that collectively comprise an "I," and we identify ourselves with these ideas. For instance, we have predefined situations that would cause us to feel sad or happy. We do not like some people or some things. We have fears and anxieties, needs and desires, sensitivities and many other external and internal expressions. The question is whether these attributes are the same ones we were born with, and if so, have they preserved their qualities? Do our present fears, envies, level of happiness or unhappiness, likes or dislikes, needs, desires, and mental attributes have the same characteristics as those that were part of our nature when we were born, or are they the product of our conditioning?

The *essence* of our inner states is unknown to us. We see a child who is genuinely happy, sad, scared, or jealous; but we are totally unaware of the root causes of such expressions. However, we can clearly see certain attributes in those states. *First, the authentic inner states are not in the domain of thought,* so when a child is in a state of fear, his thought does not suggest to him to be fearful. A child may exhibit expressions of passion and love, happiness or unhappiness, but the child is not aware of those expressions by thought or through the process of thinking. When a child shares food with another, based upon an inner desire, the child's thought does not tell him/her to be generous, or if there is no such desire, the child would not label him or herself as tightfisted. This means that for a child, there is no connection between the expression and thought. Let's look at the inner meaning of this poem by Rumi:

هر چه گویم عشق را شرح و بیان

چون به عشق آیم خجل باشم از آن

گرچه تفسیر زبان روشنگر است

لیك عشق بی زبان روشن تر است

*Much I describe love in words and interpretations,*
*When to its presence, I am in shame and regret.*

*Words of the tongue make apparent,*
*Though wordless love is more transparent.*

Love is a spiritual state that cannot be described in words. To describe something, first we would have to have knowledge of it, and "thought" is the agent of knowing. As love is not in the domain of thought, it is beyond its reach. Thought cannot explain love; love is ineffable. When we are in a state of love, we cannot *think* about this state of being. Only when that state is removed, can there be thoughts about it.

When a state has passed, whatever thought may conceive of that state, it is no longer present. There is only a memory of it. For instance, if you experience anger or fear, the moment you become aware of it or have any thoughts about it, that state has already passed. Its *content* does not remain in you, and only-mental images of that state are registered in your memory. Now thought is in connection with those images, but not with the actual state. Whatever is in the domain of thought is not a state. Thought and state do not coexist. There can only be a state without thought or a thought without a state.

*Another attribute of the human essence is that its existence and its fulfillment are not dependent on external actions.* There are states in a child that we call love, joy, humility, or generosity. Whether the child acts with generosity or not, these states naturally exist within him/her. But attributes such as generosity, courage, or humility, which you and I would consider desirable, do not have those qualities. The origins of those attributes do not come from an inner state. Instead they are dependent upon our actions and behaviors. (Actions and behaviors are based on our interpretation of subjects and circumstances.)

For instance, if you don't perform any act of bravery, you cannot tell yourself what a brave person you are. Or, if you do not give, you cannot tell yourself what a generous person you are. It is necessary for you to perform an action first, and then based on your mental patterns, you would put an interpretive label on those actions. Then, you can say that you have such and such a quality. *But the existence of authentic inner states is not dependent on whether an action is involved.*

A lion has an inherent quality that we call "courage," and this quality is always a part of the lion's makeup. However, a lion does not need to dominate another animal to obtain the label of "courageous." (We have also extended our interpretive ways to indescribable states within animals.)

26

# HOW THE "I" GETS CREATED

*Another attribute of our natural inner state that is disguised in the previously mentioned above attributes is that they are real.* Feelings like fear, humility, or generosity are real human states, even if they are indescribable, and yet we are unaware of their essence. Whereas our present mental identity has no content other than images based on words and interpretations. How do you suppose you can credit yourself with attributes like courage or generosity? Look carefully at how these attributes get created in your mind. Twenty years ago, you gave some money to someone. Your mother was witness to that action. She told you what a generous person you are. That interpretation in words has been registered in your memory, and now you credit yourself according to those words, namely that you are generous.

So, if in the above case, instead of your mom your father was present, and he told you what a dumb person you are to give without any reason, then what quality would you consider that you possess? Obviously, the "dumb" quality would be the first choice. You cannot find any attribute in your present identity—hereafter referred to as *"thought identity"*—that is not a by-product of conventional and mutually agreed upon social contractual agreements.

By now I hope you have a better understanding of how interpretive values create an "I." Here, we are not talking about true spirituality. We are discussing a phenomenon that is a *shadow* of true spirituality. To be more precise, this phenomenon is not even a shadow of our true spirituality, it is made of conventional words devoid of any inner meaning, and as such do not carry the slightest resemblance to true spirituality. *When we talk about the "I" as a harmful and destructive phenomenon, we are referring to that aspect of our minds and psyches that we are aware of through our thoughts.*

Presently, we have certain spiritual states and qualities that are part of our innate substance. But since these states are not in the domain of thought, they are not part of the composition of "I." We call a phenomenon by the name of "I," whose place is in memory, and it survives by chewing on thought like an animal chews its cud. In fact, this phenomenon called "I" is a psychological process alien to who we truly are, and it is the cause of all human suffering.

So far we've learned that one of the most important characteristics of our mental identity is its thinking nature; meaning that our identity is based in thought, and it continues its life by hanging on to thought. More precisely, this entity is exactly like thought. "Thought" and "I" are the same thing and the same process.

Now, let's examine what problems get created from the thought-based "I." The first problem that arises from thought identity is that it divides and takes away from the unity of our relationships with each other, with life, and even with our own existence, and limits all of life to a mold constructed of thought. Before our acquaintance with interpretation, we have certain states and qualities that are not conscious by way of thought. Therefore, no such "center" exists as a dividing factor in our minds. In such a state, we see ourselves as part of the entire existence. It's even more accurate to say that we do not see and feel ourselves as separate from the rest of existence because no "self" yet exists. There is only a holistic awareness of existence,

28

of which we inherently know we are a part. However, after the formation of a thought-based "center" (an "I") we see ourselves as separate from everything. On one side is the "I" or the "center," and on the other side is the rest of all that exists. The "I" sees itself as a separate entity from the whole of existence and looks at that existence as an alien "other." Our sense of separation and loneliness begins from this deep, philosophical perspective. I think the human experience of separation is an effect of this process, as Rumi points to in this poem:

منبسط بوديم و يك گوهر همه

بى سر و پا بديم آن سرهمه

يك گهر بوديم همچون آفتاب

بي گره بوديم و صافى همچو آب

چون بصورت آمد آن نور سره

شد عدد چون سايه هاى كنگره

كنگره ويران كنيد از منجنيق

تا رود فرق از ميان اين فريق

*We were joyous, all from the same treasure,*
*No heads or tails, all one piece there, by any measure.*

*Like the Sun, we were all one jewel,*
*No knots, clear as water in the pool.*

*Pure light of soul appeared in facial wonders,*
*Pinnacle shadows were cast, divided in numbers.*

# THE POWER OF NO THOUGHT

*Destroy them pinnacles with ballista provided,*
*Till are gone differences from among the divided.*

A spiritual state is like an unquantifiable light. It is without "belonging-to" and "not-belonging-to." It is without the "I." The "I" that says "such and such" specialties belong to me. It would be more accurate to say that the *quality of unity* is the essence of a spiritual state.

The nature of a spiritual state is unity, but once it falls under the domain of thought and gets divided, quantified, and named, it loses its unity and as such creates a sense of separation and loneliness. Prior to this division, we did not have any perceived dichotomy between "me and you," "me and him," "me and the truth," or "me and God." But later, when thought conjured up a center called "I," this center became the instrument of discrimination and conflict. And what lies behind this conflict is a deep sense of fear. We find ourselves isolated and lonely, facing a strong current of anger, hatred, and desire to harm others.

It is imperative to explain a point here. What we said above regarding thought, and how it interferes with the spiritual state and ruins the quality of unity, is not a precise explanation. Thought has nothing to do with the true spiritual state. Thought does not know that state, it cannot reach it, least of all to interfere with it. But thought intrudes upon our natural state in another way. Thought does not allow our lives to be lived from our true spirituality. Instead, thought takes over that role and presents a false and idealistic identity that dominates our entire lives. This false identity as thought is what causes separation. Human beings become so absorbed with thought identity that

30

they are automatically alienated from the authentic spiritual state.

*The first problem derived from thought identity is the separation of human beings from the unity of existence.* This gives them a sense of individuality, despair, powerlessness, and deep loneliness. Before the formation of this experience, human beings were part of Existence and were as large as Existence, without thinking about largeness. But, after the formation of the "thought mold,"[2] human beings feel lonely and powerless. That feeling is as small as the mold itself. Because we see ourselves as a "mold," and since that mold is shaped by thought, we perceive ourselves as a small and limited entity.

So far, we have learned that thought identity first takes us away from our natural state, then cuts off our relationship with "unity." *This creates another problem that causes the mind to partition and fragment.*

Before the formation of thought identity, the mind had an all-encompassing quality, like looking in a full-length mirror in which one can see everything. But after the mind becomes a place of hundreds of images and perceptions about the "I," it gets fragmented and always functions as an agent of one of many "Is."

To understand this better, let's look at our own thought processes. You might think that "you" are a humble person, and a moment later you might think that "you" are a selfish person.

---

[2] The author is using "thought mold" or "mold" to refer to thinking patterns and thought forms are infused in humans from an early age, which in time, encourage us to relate to each other and the external world through these thought molds.

Later still, you might think that "you" are an unsuccessful person. You, as a human being by nature, are an all-encompassing and whole entity. But when you look at yourself through the eyes of the fragmented "I," you only see a part of all that you are, separated from the whole. The moment you say, "I am inferior" or "I am incapable," you are allowing the "I" fragment, a part defined by the attribute, "inferiority" or "incapability," to represent the whole. This is what I mean when I say that our mind's mirrors are broken. Human views life and its affairs by way of the "I," and if the "I" is fragmented, i.e. it is made of individual and partial thoughts, whatever is seen through this medium is also fragmented and partial.

Imagine somebody is standing in a vast desert and is freely looking all around. Now imagine a person in a small room with no windows, but only peepholes to the outside world. The person can see outside only through one peephole at a time. Our thought mold is like that small room with hundreds of peepholes. At any given time, we are allowed to use only one peephole to view the outside world.

The human being, who looks at life through his "thought mold," can never understand the true meaning of life or learn anything of substance from life. The human mind is always preoccupied with one of the "Is," and is always floundering in the claws of the last "I." When we are caught up in a specific "I," we find such anxiety, desperation, and entanglement that we are not able to think of anything but what that specific "I" imposes on us. Being slave to individual "Is" is the usual affair. During a lifetime, we always look and relate to living through one of the "Is," with the last "I" being the most dominant at any given time.

As a result, we develop a highly fragmented view of life and the world around us. We view all life, which is interrelated and in flux, as a series of disconnected "single occurrence" events and circumstances. For example, you are a whole entity, but from my perspective you might be generous since you lent me some money. Therefore, I can never see and know you in the totality of yourself. I would tend to relate mostly to your facet of generosity.

The human who looks at life through the prism of the "I," perceives only a subset of what life has to offer. This is like a student that every hour goes to a different session with a different teacher and a different subject. That student enters a classroom in the middle of a subject, spends a few minutes there, and then goes to another classroom. Such a person cannot truly learn anything. Learning is only possible by having a "whole mind" and a perspective with a connected view, not by a mind with fragmented view.

It can be said without exaggeration that a human being who is solely identified with thought learns nothing from life. Of course, we accumulate a lot of knowledge, we learn things like sciences, technologies, and manners, but that is like second hand information received from others and stored in memory. We may have even gained extensive knowledge by looking at life through peepholes, but that does not mean our minds have true learning qualities. In true learning, quantity is not as important as the quality. A true learning mind is constantly in a state of learning, without getting attached to that which it learns. This type of learning is observation without accumulation. Therefore, whatever this mind knows, it knows it truly and authentically. (We will have a more in depth discussion about true learning in a later chapter.)

Thought identity not only partitions the mind and causes us to see the interrelated movements of life as tiny single occurrences, but it also deprives the mind of a realistic view in general. This means that when we view life through a mold of thought, it is like projecting an image from the mind onto real things and then presuming that we see reality. The generosity attribute I might see in you is merely a reflection of my own mental image.

The process of looking at life through the lenses of an "I" and its fragmented views causes two fundamental problems: The first is ignorance (by not seeing everything as part of the whole existence and relying only on the limited view of an "I.") The second is that we see life through a lens of conflict and discord in regards to relationships among human beings. The interpretive view, constructed by thought identity, is a fundamentally imaginary view. This means ignorance at a level deeper than the mind. Whatever the subject may be, such a view cannot be reality but only a shadow that the mind has cast upon reality. The conflicts and discords of human beings are derived from this imaginary or molded view. You do a specific action and interpret it with your own specific thought patterns. I do the same action with my own thought patterns, which are different from yours, and then see and interpret it all in a different way. Then, since each of our thought patterns is like a ruler of our mental existence, we don't allow ourselves to doubt the ruler's authenticity, and we defend our thought patterns with biases and hostility. Defending these different and opposing patterns brings about war, conflict, and discord among us.

We said that the human being looks at the external world and himself through a mold of preconceived ideas. And we know this mold is a phenomenon preserved by memory, meaning it resides in the memory. It is also true that whatever is in the memory is subject to aging. From thirty years, forty years, or just an hour ago—it makes no difference—images have been registered in our memories and we adopted that collection as our identity. For fifty years you may have been repeating in your mind, "I'm a pitiful person, I'm an incapable person, and I'm a disadvantaged and unsuccessful person."

Not only are these repetitive memories subject to aging, they actually make us old because they keep us living in the past. We look at new environments and a changed world through the lenses of these old and dead perceptions of what once was. Therefore, all our affairs tend to feel old and dead. It would not be an overstatement to say that from the time we adopted thought identity, we no longer had the ability to see life as new or to sense life's freshness.

Life is dynamic. Life is constantly renewing. But we view life through the outdated and obsolete instrument of the "I," or thought identity, and consequently our views are always tainted with the colors of these old mechanisms. Suppose yesterday or even thirty years ago, I had seen you perform a specific action such as showing generosity towards somebody. At that time an image of you was registered in my memory as a generous person. First of all, my mind captured those images based on my own mental patterns. Secondly, today, tomorrow, and a thousand other tomorrows I will see you through the lens of all those old images. That means I basically see you as a fixed entity.

My view about myself also has such characteristics. For forty years I've been compromising and enduring old behaviors nested within me.

Now, is this not a critical problem of the human condition? I don't know if you've noticed how restless we are! How we run away from ourselves, constantly looking for new activities and entertainments! These are all due to the fact that we internally feel a sense of boredom and dullness. If it were not for the entertaining ideas that constantly keep our bored existence busy, we would have smelled the stench of the "I" as well. In addition to staleness, thought identity also has a mechanical and stereotypical quality, whereas abiding in the natural state is rejuvenating. A child's state is continuously changing from moment to moment. However, after the mechanisms of valuation and comparison are registered in the child's mind, replacing authentic natural states, the child's being is transformed to a mechanical, mimicking, stereotypical system that always acts in accordance with the movements of specific buttons (meaning specific values.) If there is any variety in his behavior, it's a variety of value-buttons.

All these processes and conditionings indicate that we lose our inner freedom and become slaves to forms externally imposed upon our minds. Our identities were imposed on us from early childhood when we did not have the power of discernment. As human beings with thought identities, we have neither freedom nor clear seeing in any aspects of our lives, including thinking, desiring, and feeling. We go through life blindfolded.

# HOW THE "I" GETS CREATED

We do not have the power to examine anything realistically as our thought identity dominates our free thinking and renders us unconscious.

***

**Q:** *You are saying that after the dominance of thought identity, the free and conscious man turns into an unconscious and conditioned human being. The fact is that the human being in his natural state is not free and conscious anyway. If I am naturally rough or gentle, I have not chosen those qualities. Is there any reason, in the absence of thought identity, that we could not be free and conscious?*

**A:** From a philosophical point of view you are right. From a deeper perspective, a human being may feel that he/she must be sometimes rough or gentle depending on circumstances. However, we do not always think about the actions we take; those forces are a part of our nature, too. For example, your innate aggression might be a part of your being, but your present aggression has roots in the "I" that get imposed upon you externally. For instance, the infused aggression might be considered by your society to be a symbol of power.

**Q:** *Your argument applies to thought identity, too. You are saying that since we are not conscious of thought identity, we must follow it. But our present situation seems completely normal to us. We think that's the way life is supposed to be.*

**A:** Yes, in some ambiguous and unconscious way we feel that we must follow thought identity. However that feeling has become habitual in us. When we are told to eradicate this inauthentic and corruptive identity in order to live peacefully and genuinely, our first response is "I cannot." Doesn't saying, "I cannot," indicate that we feel we must follow our identity? Don't we feel that we have to live with this so-called gift, meaning thought identity?

But your other question was about consciousness. You asked why a human being without thought identity is a conscious person. It's simply because unconscious factors do not exist in that person and they have not clouded the mind. A conscious person's mind is in a direct relationship with reality and sees everything as it really is without imposing mental constructs. This is consciousness.

**Q:** *You're saying that we should look at our behaviors and that of others as they really are, meaning we should not interpret those behaviors as good or bad, or as having value or not having value. With this perspective, my question is, what is the role of "upbringing"? Without imposing values, doesn't the subject of upbringing get principally negated? Suppose a child is naturally rough and bullies other children, while another child is naturally defenseless and does not defend himself when he is bullied. How should we rectify these two behaviors? If we do not teach a child the necessity of self-defense, wouldn't he be raised as a pushover?*

**A:** Your questions indicate that the two types of views we are talking about are still not clear to you. First of all, there is no creature that does not defend itself. Every creature instinctively has the means to defend itself. When children feel the necessity to defend themselves, they will automatically and naturally do so in some way. Let's assume that a child does not defend him or herself, and we want to teach this child the need for self-defense. Do you think that we should teach this child to defend "human existence" or "value existence"?

**Q:** *Let's forget about value existence; the child should defend its human existence.*

**A:** We may say forget about value existence, but secretly our whole attention is pointed to the value existence. If we were considering the human existence, I would say that it is better to teach the child to run away when he or she is under attack and harassment. Is it not our objective to protect the child's "human existence" from harassment? Therefore, by escaping, that objective is fulfilled. What is your opinion about "escape" as a way of defense?

**Q:** *But later the child will turn out to be a weak, miserable, timid person.*

**A:** Do you notice how your viewpoint is naturally toward the child's "value existence" and not the "human existence"?

Anyway, my point is that you can have whatever type of upbringing you would like in relation to a child, but try not to allow interpretive labels to get stuck in the child's mind. Do not set up the child's mind to be a nest of both hypothetical and face values. Teach the child to defend him or herself, but the quality of this teaching should not be such that after self-defense an image of "I am brave and courageous" gets registered in the mind.

**Q:** *If we do not teach a fearful child that fear is a bad thing, isn't there a possibility that when the child grows up, the state of fear will remain in the child? I do not mean the interpretive meaning of fear, but the fear itself may stick in the child.*

**A:** First of all, we cannot say that fear is a bad thing. Fear is also a natural human state. Fear is a natural reaction to a real danger; and in fact fear has a role to sound the alarm if need be. If we did not have this natural reaction, we could not feel danger. The reason that we have a negative perception about fear is that from childhood, fear has been presented to us as valueless and pitiful. And now we are afraid of the perception of "being fearful" more than the actual fear. Secondly, suppose that fear really is an undesirable state. There's no point in proving that it is undesirable because being desirable or undesirable has no effect on the matters we're discussing here.

You are saying that if we do not tell the child that fear is bad, then it's possible that the state of fear will remain in the child. Let's see if this is correct. The child has some regular states that are a part of his spiritual substance, as well as other states that may be created accidently or due to specific factors. Once those factors are eliminated, these states will be gone automatically. Before a child enters a dark area or hears a horrible noise, the child is not in a state of fear. As soon as the child enters a dark area, a state of fear is created. After the child leaves the dark area, that state of fear is gone, and the child will be back in a normal state. Hence, fear is the effect of a cause. Once that cause no longer exists, the fear no longer exists. The "state of fear" that you say remains in the child's mind is not the actual state of fear, but an image of a valueless timid child.

We are all constantly in a state of fear, a fear of an imaginary incident. So, are these constant fears and anxieties due to real dangerous factors? Obviously they are not. Our fears are derived from our presumed values being exposed to danger. At any moment, we think a disaster may happen to our dear values. We are scared of words like "timid," "impotent," "incapable," "pitiful," and similar things, more than we are scared of actual danger. I am not afraid that you might slap me, but I fear I might find an image of myself that says, "What a defenseless person you are."

Again, let's assume that fear, self-pity, and inadequacy as such, actually are not desirable qualities that we need to live with. If there were not a center in the mind named the "I," we would not suffer much, provided that we were conscious of those qualities. If there were not a phenomenon named the "I," we would not attach to ourselves, for instance, the undesirable quality of fear, meaning that we would not take the fear personally. We would deal with fear like any other creature would, perhaps instinctively.

Do fear, self-pity, and other problems that currently exist within me cause you pain and anxiety? Certainly not. If you were to look at yourself without the interpretive perspective of the "I," then problems seem bearable and not stressful, as if those problems existed in somebody else. (Note: we are talking primarily about psychological problems here, not physical, though the topic is somewhat valid in regard to physical problems as well.

**Q:** *If we were not to have the "I," the problems of other people might still be causing us pain. Is this correct?*

**A:** That's correct. But in that case, the problem is the problem of *being human*, not the problem of the "I." The pain derived from that situation would also have an impersonal quality, which is totally different from our present relationship to pain. Actually, pain is not the right word to describe such a state. Perhaps the "feeling of empathy" is more precise.

**Q:** *In my opinion many of these conventional values are useful and necessary. For example, what is the harm in human beings showing generosity, humility, or self-sacrifice when those actions are based on a value or a means of competition? And if those values didn't exist, how would it be possible to distinguish between good and bad?*

**A:** After values are registered in the mind they form a center that basically has a destructive, mischievous, and vicious quality; and that center uses all values as means for trouble. It is possible to observe an assumed and insignificant usefulness to some values, but ultimately, at a broader level, all values bring impairment and harm. You may donate a thousand dollars to a charity based on generosity, but observe that there is not just one value that exists in you. The value of "being smarter than others" is also a part of you, as well as many more. In order to acquire a certain value like wealth, you might do anything, by any means, to achieve it, sometimes with utmost relentlessness and aggression. Having gained more wealth, you may then donate ten thousand dollars to a charity from your million-dollar wealth, in order to gain even more value.

Now let me ask you this: In principle, what problem is there in being generous without registering the act of generosity in your mind? Donate, but do not make an "I" from your action. Just donate a thousand dollars and then close the case in your mind; do not establish a mental relationship with that action. When your mind designates a meaning to your donation, such as "you are a generous person," then the "I" becomes more important than the actual act of donating. In that case, the donation is not that important to you, but rather the "I" as a donor becomes what's most important. You think about the value and not the actual act. If you felt that the act of generosity would not gain you any value, perhaps you would not donate.

Hence, you are in fact not donating; you are bartering— giving money to get value. An act of giving based on the natural human desire to give is free of expectation for reciprocity and return, whether materialistic or non-materialistic. A child does not share his toy with another child with the intention that someday the other child will do the same for him, or that others will tell him what a generous person he is. The child gives because he has the desire to give. Generosity, humility, self-sacrifice, virtue, and any other qualities have authenticity and substance when they happen spontaneously and without thought consciousness. Thought virtue, thought humility, thought generosity and thought of self-sacrifice are not virtues; they are staged acts for the purpose of bolstering one's sense of worth.

Your other question was, "If we are not bound to values, how do we discern between good and bad?" I do not say that there are no real criteria for what has value and what doesn't, or that everything is the result of some social contract or agreement. There are many circumstances and phenomena that may inherently and certainly have a desirable or undesirable quality. But the attributes "value" and "valueless" have no principle relation to "desirable" and "undesirable," and if they do, it's with a conventional shadow of those matters. What I am saying is let us remove the shadows from our minds so that we can directly approach the reality of any "desirable" or "undesirable" circumstance.

**Q:** *How can we get rid of this "fake identity"?*

**A:** Let's not be in a hurry. We'll get deeper into this later. For now let's just pay attention to the fact of this fake identity to the degree that we become aware of its aggravation. The goal of our present discussion is to show that aggravation. Since we are so accustomed to this fake identity, we do not commonly see the severity of the problem. From childhood, we have been growing up with this so-called gift called identity, and we have been constantly infused with the idea that this gift is precious and necessary. We are also so attracted to, infatuated with, and preoccupied by this identity that we have never taken the time to directly examine it. If we do that we will see that this gift is not only worthless, it is also an obstacle to our happiness. When we find clear and deep insight into its troublesome attributes, *it will disappear effortlessly* on its own, without struggle.

# CHAPTER THREE

# ARE WE AFRAID OF THE NOW?

I n the previous chapter we examined many attributes of thought identity and the problems that result from it. In this chapter we will go deeper into this discussion, and I will begin it by posing this question: *What is the natural function of thought, and does thought fulfill its function?*

As a tool, the natural function of thought is to manage the alignment of human relations with the material world. In order to build a house, to know about the atom, to learn how our bodily organs work, to go to the moon, and to resolve other problems, we need to think. However, thought, in addition to its activities in the domain of material problem solving, has also assumed a superfluous and meddling role that is not at all necessary for its functioning. This superfluous activity interferes with non-material, otherworldly, and spiritual affairs.

Thought has interjected itself into subjects such as soul, God, love, truth, and other similar matters. But, thought is not capable of understanding the essence of such subjects. The origin of thought is in the brain, and the brain is matter, and matter can only know its own kind, nothing else. Spiritual phenomena (currently the subject of our discussion), whatever quality and substance it may have, is not in the domain of thought and thought cannot know its essence.

Therefore, when we put thought in charge of managing our spirituality, we employ a completely wrong tool and create an improper means by which to relate to ourselves and to life. Thought interferes with spirituality, and its effort to know and manage the spiritual aspect of our beings is as futile, unsuitable, and erroneous as expecting our function of hearing to originate in our hands.

This brings us to an essential question: If thought is alien to the spiritual states, and it cannot know them, then what is this phenomenon (the "I") that we consider as our mental identity? It's clearly evident that the "I" is in the domain of thought. But, what is the true nature of the "I," and what trace of real spirituality might it contain?

Each human state has a quality of unknown content. A term, a word, or a symbol *represents* that state and provides a face for that state. For instance, the state of love describes the quality and the essence of spirituality, yet the word love is only a representative of that essence. As previously mentioned, thought is unfamiliar with the essence and quality of the spiritual states. Thought may retain an image of a spiritual state, but it is unable to know the content of that state. Therefore, whoever has made a spiritual identity from thought, in truth, is a hollow human being. Such a human being is nothing but a collection of terms and words.

But thought that has woven an empty notion and presented it to us as our spiritual existence, does not sit idle. Since an early age, thought has become a clever instrument of mischievousness and deception. In order to whitewash the problem of our emptiness, thought comes up with plots and tricks to keep us unaware of this truth. All of these corrective and compensatory strategies employed by the mind occupy a major portion of our thinking. Therefore, inquiry is needed to carefully examine these tricks and become familiar with them.

One of the tricks of thought is to cover up its own emptiness. (Note: "thought" and the "thought identity" are the same phenomenon and the result of the same process.) Thought does this by associating itself with a series of real or imaginary phenomena (events, circumstances, incidents, theories etc.) and then claims certain kinship with those. It is through such integration that thought attempts to disguise its emptiness. In other words, thought imagines itself to be the same as, and identical to those phenomena.

For example, say that you have studied and memorized Karl Marx's theories. Then, from those theories, you have spun an identity for yourself. In essence, what you are saying is that since Marx's theoretical system is real, then your identity, which is made of the same theories, is also real. You are now an intellectual, a committed revolutionary, and a promoter of science. Someone else does the same thing with Jean Paul Sartre's, Friedrich Hegel's, or somebody else's theories. Another person may feel a kinship with, and establish a relationship between, themselves and money, themselves and their job, themselves and their country or family. *This creates a vague notion that since money, job, country, and family are real, so is one's identity.*

Heaven only knows what kind of problems this process breeds! How do you think wars and conflicts start between you and me? What do you think is the cause of wars between nations that consist of individuals like us? If you have created an identity for yourself from Marxist viewpoints, and I have made an identity from another's viewpoints, then outwardly each one of us is in defense of our righteousness, and inwardly, in defense of our self-identities, and the result is that we slaughter one another!

Another trick of thought is to paint the empty words that constitute our identities as real, and then to encourage us to take action based on those words, and then to convince us that since the actions are real, so too are the attributes represented by those words. For example, I may give money to a friend and my friend says, "You are very generous." However, my action may not be indicative of an authentic generosity. As mentioned previously, if an attribute is authentic, there is no need for any action and external manifestation. Of course, that does not mean it does not manifest; it means an authentic attribute still exists even without being manifested. But thought-based attributes are always based on action. You do an action first, and then you stick a label on it based on your own mental patterns. You think since the action is real, the label that your mind sticks on it is also real.

One of the reasons for restlessness in human beings is that we think the more action we take, the more we exist, and that action gives us a richer identity. The cause of our restlessness, striving, and regular excuses is a psychological need to feel that we exist. We are like a person who feels cold and moves up and down to keep warm. When we try to be psychologically quiet, we may feel that we do not exist. Consequently we consider all of our striving back and forth in life as necessary to our existence. However, at a deep and fundamental level we are unaware of the stillness that exists within us. This is because the goal of our activities is always to seek for things that fulfill our desires. And since what we normally consider to be the self is a phenomenon based on illusion, all our striving and searching are also false and ultimately futile.

Another trick of the mind to escape the emptiness caused by thought identity is to keep itself away from anything that touches upon its true reality. By doing so, the mind avoids its most important questions, "What is the nature of thought identity?" "What is the nature of the 'I'"? This process of avoidance affects all aspects of our relationships and the events of our lives. We become weary and lose our objectivity. This only intensifies the problem of our ignorance and our lack of awareness of our true nature.

In order to successfully escape from reality, thought resorts to a few other less obvious schemes as well. One of which is to avoid inquiring into the true nature and inner meanings of words. Instead of focusing within, thought keeps itself busy with outer expressions of forms, words, labels, and terms.

For example, I wake up one morning, and I call myself a communist. The next day, I comfortably say that I have become a Muslim, or a Gnostic, or an intellectual, or any other label that is fashionable for that day. This indicates that if we were truly concerned about the inner meaning of anything in our lives, we would not be so easily able to change our positions on things and give in to our daily desires. Behind any of these words or labels resides a world of meaning. If I am to claim that I have become a "revolutionary," then I need to find out what major inner transformation has occurred within me for which the word revolutionary is but a symbolic representation. However, we do not embark on such endeavors because we are only concerned with what is apparent and superficial rather than what is actual and truthful.

Another of thought's tricks to escape reality is *that it keeps us unaware of the present moment and preoccupies us with two elusive and unreal times, namely the past and the future. Present time is the only time there is, and it's absolutely possible to experience life fully in the present moment.* The one who does not live in the present moment has lost the opportunity to live to the fullest. Whenever thought is occupied with time, whether in the past or in the future, *it is occupied with its own memory.* Thoughts about the past or the future will result in a series of expired images and elusive ideas.

Have you noticed how much we despise the present moment?! One of the reasons we are often impatient, in a hurry, confused, or feeling restless is due to the fact that we do not like the present moment. It seems as though we are in love with the future. We are waiting anxiously and impatiently for the present time to pass and the future to arrive. As soon as that future that we are so much in love with becomes now, we run away from it and think about a more distant future. Our minds never stay in the now. The mind always runs hastily to get ahead of the now. *In fact, we are extremely afraid of the "now" because reality is*

50

*what is happening in this moment,* and so we continue to over-
look reality by trying to escape to the future, a future that is
made up by our minds. We run away from here and now by going into the future and playing around in our imaginations there.

Please be aware that when I talk about time in the context of
past and future, I do not mean calendar or chronological time,
which obviously exists. What I'm pointing to is *the delusive
quality of time that the mind has created* in order to perpetuate
the existence of thought identity. (It is worthy of mention that
according to some philosophical beliefs, "time" is not real, neither the mind's imaginary creation of time nor the existence of
any kind of time that passes.) Our discussion here is primarily
about the imaginary time created by the mind.

The mind constantly moves and works along a temporally
invisible line. For instance, it moves back to yesterday, a year
ago, or forty years ago. It creates a mental file by gathering a
collection of past experiences and then brings them forward to
the present time. Then, based on an interpretation of those experiences, the mind determines one's current identity.

When the mind becomes preoccupied with itself, i.e. *with its
memory*, which is nothing but a collection of images of past experiences, a *mental-time-in-the-past* gets created. Then the mind
compares this collection with its current ideal patterns, only to
find that the collection of past images is no longer desirable and
valuable. So, the mind fancies bringing the collection closer and
matching it to its current ideal patterns by projecting its fulfillment into the future. From this process, the *mental-time-in-the-
future* gets created almost effortlessly.

By tapping into the past, which is all our accumulated

51

memories, the mind creates a sense of deficiency, loss, discontent, and disappointment, and by *jumping* into the future, the mind creates a sense of delusive greatness that simultaneously accompanies fear, despair, and envy. Then, moving forward, the mind projects an outstanding, flawless, and ideal identity into the future in which there is no trace of fear, inferiority, discontent, or other problems. But the mind has learned through experience that thousands more tomorrows have come and gone and thought identity is still the same as before. This matter causes a deep despair, a sense of regret and envy for the human being. Although we are not willing to candidly admit it, deep inside our hearts we are completely aware that hoping for a future we feel is better than the present is an illusory hope.

I mentioned that one of the essential strategies of the mind to escape emptiness and the absurdity of thought identity is to keep away from whatever is reality, including itself. So at the same time, thought introduces another interesting side tactic. It implicitly allows others to serve as proxies to shape its identity. It implicitly says, "I do not know what my identity is; *you* tell me what I am."

One of the reasons that we give extra importance to others' opinions and judgments about us is due to this process. In fact, others determine our psychological fates. Our psychological lives and deaths depend on people's opinions and judgments. For instance, if you tell me that I am an ignorant person, I believe it; or if you tell me that I am a wise person, then I believe that too. (Is there any reason clearer than this for thought identity to be based on the power we give to words?! If this entity had any true content, could it so easily get changed from one thing to another?)

In fact, becoming self-estranged and allowing others to serve as proxy to ourselves is the mind's desperate attempt to keep us ignorant of the true nature of thought identity. But this process of self-alienation gradually spreads to all aspects of our existence and we become isolated from everything in life. Our thoughts, feelings, perceptions, and sentiments undergo a radical change, becoming muddy and dull.

For example, you may have seen individuals who eat on schedule versus when they are hungry, as if, on behalf of their stomachs, they have given authority to the clock. They also apply the above rule to sleeping, sex, and other activities. They do not clearly know what they like and what they dislike. They do not know what food suits them and what does not. Bound by thought identity, we are not aware of life and cannot see things clearly. We always keep our eyes half open lest we see. Clarity is not one of thought identity's virtues.

Now, let's examine the problems that arise when we let others serve as our proxies and drag our spiritual center of gravity outside of us. Let's see how the undercurrent of thought identity attacks us from all sides, rendering us desperate and entangled.

As mentioned earlier, the rationale for the creation of thought identity is to compete and get ahead of others. But to succeed in this competition we desperately need the help of our rivals. I need to be smarter and cleverer than you so that I can use those qualities as weapons against you. But the factor that is expected to confirm my qualities of intelligence and cleverness is you. By the same token, it would not be prudent to extend any help to me because it would be against your self-interest. You are, in fact, my rival, and any confirmation of my value indicates the negation of your own. Because we know this, it is only through comparison that we can imagine a conventional value within us.

Often in our relationships with others we are more negative and destructive than positive and constructive. This is a reality that we can clearly observe in our relations. In order to make you to doubt your value, I might resort to belittling, condescension, and other negative tactics. I use waspishness, pedantry, friendly advice, and sarcastic language. I downplay values that you believe in. I try to make you feel inadequate by boasting about my job, furniture, fancy house, and cleverer and smarter kids. Sometimes by pretending to be wisely silent I might create doubt in your mind about your value and put myself in a better position in comparison to you. Despite constantly putting on a show of our highest human qualities, and despite all the polished justifications and excuses that we invent to disguise our undesirable behaviors, we can clearly see that all our behaviors and relationships are tainted with destructive and malignant tendencies.

It is obvious that under such circumstances, we cannot have the feeling of cooperation, love, and brotherhood with each other. Psychological need or "value-based" need is destined for fear and hatred, which are the enemies of love. You and I desperately need each other's help. But at the same time we both try to deprive each other of the same with utmost frugality. Hence, our relationships are fundamentally inharmonious, rough, and full of discord. We are like the beggars whose livelihoods are in the hands of others. If others do not give the beggars a handout, then their existence will be at risk, and rarely do these needs get fulfilled to their satisfaction. One of the reasons that our spirits are often down as we get older is that our value-based "food" diminishes day after day. Our passion and zeal for life gets weaker and complaining becomes one of the perpetual qualities of our existence. Obtaining a higher value is like food to our spirits.

Another trick that the mind employs to declare thought identity to be real (again, nothing but a collection of empty words) is to utilize "feelings." Thought uses words to create feelings in us such that we confuse feelings with the contents of the words. If when you were told "What a clever and wise person you are," these words did not give rise to subsequent feelings, then this means that you would not have any attachment or interest in preserving the words, and you would not be willing to accept a bunch of empty words as your spirituality. In realizing the danger of this situation, thought creates a *feeling* within us it deems suitable to the words, so that we will continue to imagine that thought identity has contents and is something more than empty words.

It is important to explain that, from a certain point of view, there are *two* types of feelings. One is feelings that are *reactions to thoughts*. The other is feelings that are *independent of thoughts*. These two different expressions can be described: Feelings whose origins come from reactions to thoughts are described as *emotions*. The non-reactionary feelings (without thoughts) are described as *sensations*.

For instance, a child may have certain feelings whose root causes are not known to us. We can only say that such feelings are not reactions to thoughts. The child is not thinking about his/her father's social status as a boss or as a famous person and then feels happy. Neither does the child think about his/her father's low status in society and then feel deprived. All of the child's feelings are non-reactionary (to thoughts,) whereas in adult human beings nearly every feeling is the result of reaction to *thoughts*. First you think that you are a boss, an artist, a famous person, and then you feel happy. Our current feelings actually guarantee the survival of the phony and empty identities that are made up of words. The reason "happiness" and "enjoyment" have reserved a very elevated place in us, so much so that we look for them in any subject or relationship, is their substitutive role.

*We have lost our original quality of joyfulness and now are searching everywhere for its replica, i.e. pleasure.* Why are pleasure and happiness so important to us? Is it not because we feel empty and unhappy inside and we want to fill this emptiness with quasi qualities in lieu of spirituality?

One of the catastrophes of thought identity is that it makes us essentially inwardly barren and seemingly soulless. In order to create some sort of quasi spirit and quasi state, we become dependent upon empty words, devoid of meaning. If you pay close attention, you will notice that your so-called psychological life revolves entirely around empty words. I have to await your confirmation that "I am a good speaker" before I feel good about myself. Consequently, my psychological existence is a borrowed existence, suspicious, shallow, and dependent.

*Rumi* says:

# ARE WE AFRAID OF THE NOW?

آنکه او بسته غم و خنده بود

او به این دوعاریت زنده بود

باغ سبز عشق کو بی منتها است

جز غم و شادی در او بس میوه هاست

*Those with lives filled with laughter and sorrow,*
*Have no choice but to live between the two, in borrow.*

*Where is the green garden of love, that's infinite?*
*More than sorrow and laughter, plenty of fruits in it.*

Our sorrow and joy are both reactive and short-lived. Whereas love—or better said, the zeal of existence—is an independent and authentic state: deep, expansive, and beyond the domain of thought.

To summarize: Thought, by interfering in the affairs of spirituality, not only has abandoned its principal function, i.e. aligning our relationship with the material world, but also it has tried and failed to grasp our true spirituality. We are bestowed with two precious gifts that clearly distinguish us from other living beings. One is the gift of thought; the other is spirituality. Human thought, as far as we know, is much stronger and broader in range than it is in other creatures. Human brain cells, and the source of thought, are richer in both quality and quantity than in other sentient beings. If thought were to function only at the level of its chartered duties, heaven knows how it could support our progress and evolution as human beings. We have not used our thinking properly. Thought has a useful role and purpose that is part of human existential structure. But we have wasted that beneficial quality and converted it into a destructive tool with mischievous and deceptive motivations. More importantly, with our thoughts meddling and interfering in our spirituality, the gift of our spirituality is tainted as well. Thus, our attention must be focused on restricting our thoughts to their designated domain and restoring our spirituality. This is achieved through an "unlearning" process that will be presented in the coming chapters.

\*\*\*

**Q:** *In my opinion, true human beingness and the society that you describe are desirable; but reaching that destination would be extremely difficult, if not impossible. How many people do you think exist in the world with the characteristics that you describe?*

**A:** Why should we view this subject this way?! To know how many people have reached that state is not going to help us. (Again, please pay attention to how "comparison" in any process is dominant over our view and mind!) Why should we bother knowing if others have reached that state or not.

We have all been conditioned to believe that life is about childish amusements, vain and perpetual struggles, fears and anxieties that continuously grind down and dampen our spirits. However, now you are hearing of another possibility. I am encouraging you to pay attention to your life, and to understand that your life is very unstable, shallow, empty, and vulnerable. It's as if we have built our existence in a swamp, but now we can realize that we are living false lives, devoid of meaning. It is imperative that we free ourselves from the grips of this false-hood called thought identity, and to let our authentic nature rule our lives.

At this point I do not ask whether others have freed them-selves from the "I." For instance, if you lost your child, you would desperately look everywhere to find him. You would not be thinking about others who might have lost their children and didn't look for them, or who have looked for them and have not found them. This is about your own dear child. This is a serious and fundamental problem, not who has found a lost child or not! Our problem is that we still have not felt the urgency of what we have lost and how we have replaced a precious one with a worthless one.

**Q:** *Isn't it idealistic to seek for such a thing?*

**A:** First of all, "seeking" is a vain effort. The example of "searching for the lost child" only symbolizes the urgency of the matter. Any type of search or any action orchestrated by thought takes us a step further into the entanglement of thought identity (and I will clarify this more fully in future discussions.)

For now, let's see what we mean by "ideal." In my opinion, one meaning of ideal is when someone thinks of a utopian and unreal existence. In other words, one searches and desires some-thing that does not presently exist. Another meaning of ideal is "perfection." This means to think and to want matters to be flawless, impeccable, and absolute. Well, considering the above explanations, is what I am saying idealistic, or is it the way we currently conduct our lives? My point is seeing and accepting you and your life *as they are*. Do not chase anything other than what you are, and do not desire another thing. Do not live for tomorrow. Do not look at life through interpretive glasses.

In contrast, you are saying that since people have lived for years and centuries with those mental interpretations, and since this type of living is what exists therefore it must be preserved. If someone were to say, "Let us live without interpretation," then that person has uttered an idealistic statement! If you enter a town and see that everyone is going about with their eyes closed, and then you suggest to them that they open their eyes to see life clearly, have you made an idealistic statement?

**Q:** *It seems to me that first of all, you think the human personality is the result of thought and imagination, and you do not consider there to be any real validity there. Secondly, you summarize the human spiritual existence, which is very complex, as something valuable or valueless; whereas we know that human beings have sentiments that have nothing to do with "value." We have desires, instincts, needs, specific characters, and many other things, none of which is based on value or the result of thought and imagination.*

**A:** I do not know whether I explained the problem of "real view" and "mental view" in an ambiguous and convoluted form, or if you do truly desire to understand my point?! You see, my dear; I do not say human sentiments, desires, and instincts are the result of imagination. I say the "I" itself is the result of imagination. The "I" is not and cannot be made up of spirituality; rather it is made up of the shadow of spirituality. Our whole talk and discussion is about this *shadow*.

Let's look at a particular case, and perhaps it will clarify what I mean by "real view" and "mental view."

The other day a woman told me: "I was at a party and I saw

a couple of other women pointing to my husband and saying what a hopeless addict he is. When I heard this, I felt so embarrassed and ashamed that I wanted to be devoured by the earth." Then, someone else present asked her, "Why did that upset you? We know that drug addiction really harms one's health. For example, it damages the lungs, contaminates the blood, and stains the teeth. Are you upset that your husband's addiction will destroy his lungs and teeth?" The woman answered, "No, who cares about his lungs or his teeth, I am worried about people saying that my husband is a drug addict."

This is a good example of what I mean by "real" views as opposed to "mental" views. I am saying that if we look at drug addiction as a real thing, there are only stained teeth and damaged lungs. I do not deny those as undesirable realities. But the delusional phenomenon that we consider as the "I" only cares about the shadow of those real things like the husband being identified as a drug addict.

**Q:** *Well, if we only looked at drug addiction as a reality and did not condemn it as something bad, there wouldn't be any motive for quitting.*

**A:** It is completely the reverse. Presently, our minds pay little attention to "stained teeth and damaged lungs" and are mostly preoccupied with the "drug addict" label. Therefore, we do not see and feel the seriousness of the "health damage" with our whole beings. If we were to give our attention to the "health" problem, then we would realize the depth of the aggravation, in which case it would be more likely that we'd find a remedy.

The interpretive view has a cause and effect attribute, and it is imperative to clarify this as we will certainly and frequently encounter it in future discussions. Basically, the interpretive view imposes specific ways to perceive life that are totally different from real life. From the time we first begin to experience life, all interpretive values and perceptions cause an underlying sense of falsely existing, and then we do not know any life other than this. Now, by hearing these ideas about authentic and natural living, we may begin to perceive an authentic life, yet still that perception, if it is based in thought identity, will always be incomplete and insignificant.

The mind cannot grasp the state and spiritual quality of a human being who lives an authentic life. We are like people who have been in prison their whole lives and can only *imagine* what life is like outside the prison. For example, the very question, "If we look at drug addiction as a reality, then there will not be any motivation to quit," indicates an incomplete understanding. If you were to look at the subject a little more broadly, and go through it step by step, you would notice that the root cause for escaping to drugs, cigarettes, alcohol, etc., is the interpretive view itself.

As was illustrated earlier, from the accumulation of interpretations, a center gets created in the mind called the "I." In this center, there are hundreds of substantial and troublesome problems such as feelings of self-pity and deficiency, inadequacy, fear, and envy, all of which we are usually afraid to look at. Therefore, we try to escape from them in any manner possible. One of the ways we escape is to drown ourselves in drugs, alcohol, and similar addictions so as not to see how our lives may be full of self-pity, disappointment, anxiety, and insecurity. Whereas, if we were to look at our lives and our behaviors without interpretation, the mental center with its problems would not even get created. In this case, it would not be necessary to lose oneself to drugs, alcohol, and hundreds of other amusements and activities with similar effects.

**Q:** *Let's assume that we could lose thought identity. In that case, how would our lives get managed? What would be our behavioral motivation? Presently, due to our motivation for value, we seek certain activities, behaviors, and relations. If seeking for value does not exist, what would happen to our relationships and behaviors?*

**A:** In that case, *the order that governs the whole existence* would manage our lives in a useful, harmonious, and logical way, not disorderly, messy, and metamorphic. To put it more precisely, if we were to remove the phenomena of anger and hatred from our minds, "love" would become dominant within our beings and over our lives; and love would do its magic. Living in a state of love has a quality that is obviously completely different from living in a state of anger and hatred.

We are so much accustomed to thought identity and its flashy and deceitful preoccupations and amusements that life without it seems difficult; when in fact the fabrication of an "I" is like a mental polyp. If you remove it from your mind, what remains is your authentic nature. Then true human nature will manage your life.

# CHAPTER FOUR

## THE "I" CREATES THE CONFLICT

T hought identity, in the beginning of its formation, is very simple. It presents us with certain values, and then pushes us to adapt our lives to those values, using them to move forward. But the nature of those values is such that day after day they expand and grow in complication. One fundamental cause of these complications is that thought identity is devoid of any real content. Yet, we try our best to ignore this void.

Another factor in making thought identity complicated is *conflict*. There are certain factors in the structure of thought identity that inevitably cause all kinds of conflicts. Its constantly shifting and often contradictory attributes confront its adverse and inharmonious goals, turning our existence into a stage for opposition and struggle. In this chapter, I will review these thought-generated conflicts and their attributes, as they cause the "I" to become more complex and create further difficulties.

*The first conflict that gets created after the mind establishes a system of values is the basic conflict between human nature and thought identity.* When values dominate the mind, our natural inner state is not replaced by these imposed values all at once. Our authentic self resists this imposition. Our true nature recognizes these "values" as foreign and tries to protect us from them. (Of course, none of this happens consciously. The quality of human nature necessitates such conflict.)

We are very familiar with the power of values, the strength of its infusion and its incessant repetition. Values are like invisible thick walls surrounding the mind, no matter which way we turn, we cannot escape these walls. Therefore, despite all striving, our true nature is eventually defeated and enslaved by mental values. This does not mean that our natural inner state has disappeared completely. Just beneath our conscious awareness, the inner resistance and conflict remain. Our society, with a relentless force, tries to make our inner essence surrender to the values of the "I," or thought identity. But our true nature is incompatible with these strained and artificially infused forces. The result of this incompatibility is a constant hidden clash. The conflict between our true nature and our system of values causes us to live against ourselves throughout our lives, and will always be at war. The two are incompatible with each other. Our movements are neither confirmed by our real nature nor by the "I," therefore we are always in contention and conflict within ourselves.

This conflict brings up some rooted problems consisting of a type of anger and hatred and a feeling of revolt and restlessness, as well as associated feelings of guilt and defectiveness. The feelings of anger and hatred stem from our true desire to live our natural authenticity, but in every step of our lives we find ourselves up against conventional values. Hence, we expe-

66

rience feelings of revolt, restlessness, and anger toward ourselves and whoever imposes those values on us. Gradually, the anger and hatred find a broader dimension and become a major part of our psyches.

The reason for feeling guilty is also that, on the one hand we see ourselves confronted with our authentic spirituality, and on the other hand confronted with imposed conventional values, and we know that the commanding powers of both sides are very strong. Therefore, to act in favor of either feels like a betrayal to the other and results in feelings of guilt.

*Another conflict that gets created after the mind registers values is the conflict among the values themselves.* The values that form thought identity are the result of contradictory interpretations. It is rare to get the same interpretation from the same action. Everyone interprets life and circumstances according to their mental patterns at the time, while patterns are different from person to person. As a child you do not intuitively react roughly against the aggression of another child. Your mother tells you what a nice and gentle kid you are, but then your father may tell you what an incapable kid you are. This means that one person attaches a meaningful value for not reacting adversely while another person sticks a valueless label to the same behavior. Consequently, our minds get filled with all kinds of interpretations and contradictory meanings that form our identities.

Suppose there are no contradictory interpretations from a specific action; and even so, there is still a conflict in the essence of the interpretations. Based on a specific behavior, we may tell a child, "You are a brave kid," and assign this valuable attribute to that child. Consequently, the child automatically draws a conclusion that "lack of courage" is obviously value-less. Every *mental value along with its opposite* are registered in the child's memory; and the child constantly has an eye on each side. If the child qualifies him or herself for the attribute of courage, the child then puts all its effort into preserving that and staying away from its opposite. And if the child builds a timid image of his or herself, then the child constantly tries to escape this image and to convert it to courage. The constant *thinking* about reaching and becoming indicates that the we are dissatisfied with our current image and want to convert it into its opposite. Conflict and struggle are hidden in the core of this process. The conflict between *what is* and *what should be*.

*Another extensive conflict that contributes to the intricacies of the self results from the side effects of values.* Though some values may not have an overt contradiction with another, their outcomes may result in conflict with each other. For example, one of our respected social values is that we should be clever. Another value is that we should like others and attract their friendship. These values do not have detectible conflicts with each other per se. But let's see how they clash and create conflicts within us.

To ascribe to oneself the value of being "clever," one could get involved in activities that require struggle, contention, defeat, deception, and things like that. However, to attract the friendship of others, one is obliged to show remission and gentleness, and generally to avoid any action or behavior that may bring about competition, aggression, and resentment. Since we cannot expect the friendship of others, and since we carelessly compete and fight with each other, even though the value of being "clever" does not have any conflict with the value of being "likable," in practice their outcomes will be completely conflicting.

Considering that thought identity is formed by hundreds of different values, and from every value additional results are produced, we can quickly grasp how messy and contradictory the outcome of this mixture could be. Our minds have become a clearinghouse of hundreds of different and contradictory "Is." Every one of the "Is" has pretenses, goals, desires, and needs different from the rest. One thought is in conflict with another thought, one feeling with another feeling, past with future, and they are all in conflict with the present moment. Everything in our existence is chaotic and ill-matched. Every minute we are in pursuit of fulfilling a desire, different from and contradictory to the rest.

Briefly, I will point out some of the problems raised from the conflict of values. One problem derived from conflicting values is that it causes us to lose our direction and become confused about our goals in life. A person who lives in conflict cannot act wholeheartedly in any facet of life. That person cannot desire anything seriously with their whole being. All their objectives have a "whatever happens, happens!" quality.

For instance, we say we desire freedom, but our actions and behaviors indicate that we are not serious; we do not desire freedom with our whole being. Demand for freedom is more of a nag and a preoccupation within us. We see our lack of freedom as degrading and valueless and we revolt against that. But there are many other factors in us that do not desire freedom. The desire of a person who lives authentically and acts wholeheartedly is not characterized by "Let's wait and see what happens, let's see what others say and do and then I will follow." A person who feels like a human being—not a bunch of words and concepts—whatever they desire, they want with their whole being.

Conflict causes us to feel internal despair, entanglement, and acute inadequacy. In spite of all pretentious acts to display power, inwardly we feel trapped, incapable, and helpless. When we think deeply about our feelings, we can see that all our acts, busyness, and pretenses in life are to cover our feelings of inadequacy. In some instances, we see this clearly but then immediately close our eyes. Our mood is like that of standing on the edge of a cliff and closing our eyes because of the fear that generates.

Now there is a question whose clarification would help a lot in understanding thought identity and the reasons for its complexity. That question is: With all these inner conflicts and disharmonies, how can the structure of thought identity continue its existence? When considering this curiosity, the internal chaos and conflicts in our lives must be completely crippling! Because for every feeling, thought, desire, and hope, there is one or more correspondingly opposite feeling, thought, desire, and hope. Consequently, how can we even function with all these internal oppositions going on? Yet, we see that this is not the case, and somehow we continue with our lives. Let's look at the reason for this.

Thought identity is like a governmental organization, equipped with all the necessary means for running its administration. Similar to a government headquarters, in relation to life thought identity has found a cunning quality, which is to not sit idle for a minute. Our thought identity is constantly trying to whitewash any lags or ill matches in our identity structure. The mind finds a solution for any problem to make sure of the survival of this so-called "dear" identity it has created and feels responsible to protect. It is as though thought has created a plethora of secret workers and servants who serve in various nooks and crannies of its flimsy identity to prevent its decay. It also creates legislators, policemen, interrogators, lawyers, regulators, and whatever is necessary to protect the existence of the "dear thought identity."

The main duties of these workers and servants are centered on managing conflicts. There are no factors more destructive and problematic to our happiness than conflicts in the structure of thought identity. Hence we need to investigate the roles of these workers and servants and the way they work.

One of the most common tactics for hiding our inner conflict is to use "free will," which finds a reinforcing role in the organization of our thought identity. Accordingly, when we are caught between contradictory factors and tensions, we can then take side with one of the tensions and move ourselves into alliance with it.

Please recognize that free will also exists in the person who is liberated from thought identity. However, its quality is completely different from the free will we are discussing now. The former is part of our nature and in service of our human growth. The latter is like a strap, fastening together the contradictory pieces of our thought identity. The life of a liberated person is free of impediments and entanglements. That person lives in a free-spirited and harmonious manner with all of life. The liberated person does not have to have motivation for doing things in life.

Free will operates in the domain of thought identity and indicates the existence of conflicts. For instance, suppose you want to learn a foreign language. If there are no adverse factors to distract you, you should be able to fulfill your desire very comfortably. Then, the only time you think about and resort to free will is when you are confronted with internally adverse factors and you have to decide on one factor over another.

The authentic and natural use of free will has a quality that moves us forward in a direction where our inner essence and potential can flourish; whereas our present free will is in fact the whip of whichever "I" is the strongest in the moment.

We know that in different situations, different "Is" dominate our existence. Therefore, from a philosophical point of view, we could say that we do not have free will. For example, you cannot determine to always act the same in every relationship, for instance with the determination to always be calm. Your actions depend on how a specific situation weighs on you, causing you to revert to interpretations that match your identity structure.

Those thought-generated workers and servants do not act alone; they get help from each other in doing their duties. For instance, after free will does its duty, another servant responsible for "justification" starts its job. Once, with the help of free will, we move toward one of the contradictory "Is," it's not like the case is closed. Immediately, we have to respond to opposing "Is." We have to justify our actions in whatever way possible. All justifications and rationalizations made after each action indicate that we are caught up in inner conflict. It's like something within puts us on trial as to why we've done a certain action and insists we come up with logical reasons for our actions.

For example, if we marry someone we should justify why we did it. Then if we marry someone else, we must explain our reasoning. If we do not get married at all, we feel we must justify being single. And all of this seems pretty normal to us. We cannot imagine it any other way. If I tell you that tomorrow I will go to the beach, immediately it seems as though this news is incomplete. Something's missing. It's like an inner interrogator is demanding, "You want to go to the beach? You want to *simply* go to the beach?! No, you need to justify your decision to go to the beach!" Then we get busy justifying that "Yes, the family is pushing to get away from the city because they're tired of the crowd. It's been over two years that we have not gone to the beach," etc.

Another servant of thought identity is self-blame. In fact, self-blame is like a bribe the mind uses against the opposing "Is." What is hidden in self-blame is that we are saying to those opposing "Is," "I'm sorry that I did not act upon your desires. I made a mistake. Next time I'll act in your favor. I am not satisfied with what I've done. Therefore, I deserve to blame myself."

As another example, we may not defend ourselves against an abusive insult. The act of nondefense is apparently the job of a nice "I." But within us live roughshod warrior "Is" as well, and we feel we must respond to all the "Is." Thus we blame ourselves again to keep all those "Is" satisfied.

Self-recrimination has a vast and destructive effect in our lives. The reason our spirits are often down, and the reason we do things out of regret, anxiety, and fear is that a part of us condemns whatever we've done and causes us to punish ourselves with the whip of blame and remorse. We not only blame ourselves for what we've done, we also blame ourselves for what we haven't done, for not taking action. Because conflict is part of our existence, some of the "Is" see the opposing ones as disruptive to their existence and so are always badgering us about something or other. Therefore, patterns of blame and discontent become habitual. I'm not certain a moment passes by happily in our lives without the underlying feeling of self-blame, a moment that results in mental ease and peace, where we accept our current situation unconditionally and are completely satisfied. (And do not mistake happiness with pleasure. Real happiness is a deep state that has no root in the thinking mind. Pleasure, on the other hand, is a reaction to thought; hence it is a mostly superficial kind of happiness mixed with anxiety.)

Previously it was shown that the mind, due to decomposition by the "Is," fixates on a "fragmented" or "singular" view of a given situation. The singular view is a quality automatically imposed on the mind because one's psychological existence has been formed by "single images." However, the mind knowingly uses the same single view tactic to not see the existing conflicts inherent in thought identity and thus the single view dimension is heightened. The mind intentionally tries not to understand human behavior as a connected and continuous flow so that it is not confronted with the many contradictions that exist in human behavior. The mind always tries to keep itself focused on a specific "I" in order to not pay attention to any opposing "Is." However, whenever we are caught up in a specific "I," we become so helpless and enslaved that we lose the power to look at or think about anything else. It's like each one of the "Is" at any given moment creates channels in our minds and commands us to look at our behaviors and other life circumstances only through that channel!

Have you ever heard a statement like, "In certain circumstances I get so agitated and anxious that I cannot feel my state of being?" Human beings who are slaves to the "I" have this quality. They cannot see their states of being. It's like they are in shock, suffering from amnesia, dizzied and disoriented.

A few nights ago, I was watching a television documentary with a couple of friends about wars and their human casualties. One of the friends, overtaken by so much human suffering, got very depressed and started weeping. The following day we were talking about the right of the people to have national sovereignty. The same person who was weeping the night before about the casualties of war said proudly, "One should defend one's mother land no matter what the cost." Do you notice the conflict here? It is strange that due to our fragmented views we are not conscious of such clear conflicts. As if the person who got depressed is different from the one who wants to go to war. Not seeing those obvious contradictions is due to having singular and fragmented views.

Along with these techniques, the mind employs yet another interesting trick that has a big role, and that is intentionally resorting to ignorance. Thought tries not to see anything clearly, not only in an attempt to escape from the emptiness of thought identity, but also in an attempt to escape from conflicts and hundreds of unconscious problems. It's as if the mind creates an invisible cloud around itself and tries to see life from behind that cloud. The mind's goal is to not allow us to clearly perceive the devastation of thought identity. If we had a conscious and vigilant mind, we could directly see how we have a multi-headed dragon nested within our existence, and then its life would be in danger.

***

Now I would like to clarify a couple of points that are often misunderstood and which seemingly contradict each other. For example, I have said that a person who is caught up in thought identity is an empty person. However, I might also say that such a human is very prolific. In this case I would want you to pay attention to the meaning and the content of what I am pointing you to and not necessarily the particular phrases. When I say that this person is empty, I mean that there is no real "spiritual substance" present, that this person does not have what they should have. On the other hand, this person's mind may be literally crammed full of images and words. And those words and images are the cause of a cluttered, heavy mind.

I have said that a life directed by thought identity is monotonous and stereotypical. However, I might also say that such a person is moody and inconsistent. The reason I say it's stereotypical is that whatever this person does is in the framework of the thought identity mold. The cause of the inconsistency is that the mold has a colorful quality because it's been created from hundreds of images or different "Is." Every moment we are captured by one of the "Is" and our actions are based on the commands of different "Is." Therefore, our lives are not necessarily monotonous.

Another subject that may require some clarification is the two types of views, or two types of relationships. I hope by now their actual meanings have been clarified, however, I have used some different phrases and expressions in different contexts.

For example, I have mentioned "real view" as opposed to "mental view"; "relation to what is" as opposed to "relation to what the mind creates"; and "real relationship" as opposed to "pretentious relationship" and other expressions. Now that we have become more familiar with these concepts, we can choose two expressions that sum up all the rest and I will use them throughout the rest of the book. Bear in mind, however, that no expression could comprehensively explain all attributes of the two views and the results hidden in each one. But the two expressions that most closely embody all of these attributes are "active" and "passive."

From here out I will use "passive" in place of "real" view, and "active" in place of "mental" view. We know that one of the obvious differences between "real" and "mental" views is that in the real view one lives in a state of natural being, without creating a center as the "I." However, in the mental view, a center gets created, and I refer to this as the "I." This center has an active quality, which means that it is always busy with plotting something, is always preoccupied with the self, is constantly condemning something or wanting to get rid of something, or is idealizing something and trying to obtain it, and it is continuously coming up with excuses. In short, this center is continuously striving to achieve something.

On the other hand, in the absence of the "I" center, there is no striving and no excuses. We accept ourselves and see life as it is—without trying. Naturally this way of being has the qualities of consent and acceptance. However, please note that acceptance is not indicative of an inwardly petrified or static quality. It is actually the reverse. When we allow ourselves to live from a natural state of being, we are continuously changing and growing, *without desiring this or even labeling it as* growth.

Conversely, when engaged in the active view, in spite of all our strivings and excuses, we get stuck with old images that have created walls and a mental mold from which we attempt to live. In this case, despite everything we may have created for ourselves externally, we are limited and internally imprisoned by this mental mold.

Nonetheless, from now I will use "passive" view in place of "real" view and "active" view in place of "mental" view. And though words and expressions are not important, the content is important.

***

**Q:** *Are you saying that a human being with a passive view accepts circumstances as they happen? And if so, should one accept situations where one is exploited and there are no social freedoms?*

**A:** What we are discussing here relates to psychological matters. When it comes to materialistic and physical matters, accepting those situations as they are does not have much meaning. When the roof over my head is leaking or I am hungry, and I do not try to solve these problems. I will be in trouble.

In regards to psychological matters, your question indicates that you do not have a comprehensive familiarity with the possibility of seeing life without the "I," meaning to live one's life without interpretation. This does not mean automatically accepting exploitation and injustice, nor does it mean solving those problems. Such a person innately feels free. They do not accept any lack of freedom imposed externally.

Have you ever noticed that when a piece of twig gets in one's eye, the natural defense system repels it with teardrops? Our psychological existence has a quality that links us with our natural state. Being exploited—and of course exploiting—does not suit this nature, therefore we cannot accept either. Like the twig, our nature repels these possibilities automatically and immediately, not waiting for fifty, a hundred, or a thousand years.

Freedom, justice, being exploited and exploiting are actually inner matters. External justice and freedom are expressions of inner freedom. If one is not liberated internally, and does not feel free, they do not comprehensively know the meaning of real freedom. Any kind of external freedom without inner freedom is phony, simply a feel-good reaction. Anyone who goes through life choicelessly following factors imposed by the outside does not know freedom.

The type of freedom that we see in some societies has a gamesome quality. In some countries there may no longer be dictatorship, but it has been replaced with the power of propaganda, or individual and group powers have been replaced with governmental power.

In essence, it does not make any difference if I am forced to live and to think by another's will, whether by military force or by propaganda. With propaganda my mind is put under a lot of pressure and influence, taking away my ability to think freely, and I cannot see anything other than the propaganda I've been indoctrinated with.

One day I had a discussion with a lady from the West. She said that in the Eastern countries there is not much freedom, even girls and boys cannot select their future spouses freely and instead their parents decide for them. I told her that it is the same in the Western countries, albeit with pretentious differences. My father may choose a wife for me according to his mental patterns and wishes. Your father has already imposed his mental patterns, criteria and wishes on you and now he tells you that you are free to choose your spouse according to your desires (which in fact are your father's desires.) In principle they are the same. Either way, you and I choose our spouses based on someone else's desires.

**Q:** *Is there conflict in a healthy human being, meaning one without thought identity? For example, could a child get caught up in conflict when for a moment he desires to share and then the next moment doesn't?*

**A:** Since we are accustomed to interpretation and we get to know a thing by comparing it to its opposite, then yes, different desires and states of a child, such as sharing or non-sharing, can seem contradictory. However those states do not form conflict in a child.

First of all, a child does not interpret his states so as to compare those interpretations. The child does not see sharing as generosity and non-sharing as tightfistedness, and then see them in opposition to one another. Each state has an independent quality, free from comparison and opposites.

Secondly, a child is not familiar with the concept of time and he does not create a mental file from life events. For a child, everything happens in the present time. That means a child lives in the *present*. Once a state is finished the next state comes, without having the next state be a point of comparison to the previous one. Hence, each state has a new and different quality, in itself not contradictory.

**Q:** *When one is caught up between "Is" of opposite pulls, is it not better to ignore the opposites and surrender to the power of logic, instead of relying on free will?*

**A:** Where does one get the logic from? Any logic still comes from the mold of thought identity. The mold dictates logic to us.

**Q:** *It seems to me that one cannot decide and act based on the science of logic and visible realities without being influenced by the mold.*

**A:** We could approach the problem somewhat that way if we were to deal with a scientific problem. I say "somewhat," because thought and an active view influence and even darken the mind on concrete and visible matters. Anyway, here we are talking about psychological problems. It is impossible to have a logical reflection on psychological problems in the domain of thought identity. Our thought still has a logical quality when it is in the passive mode, meaning when there is no mental activity. If the mind does not have mental activity, that means the "I" no longer exists, let alone any conflict.

THE POWER OF NO THOUGHT

**Q:** *The human being that you are describing, meaning the one who does not think about value, can that person be a responsible human being? It seems such a human being would be indifferent to and unconcerned with everything.*

**A:** It's completely the reverse. Such a human is naturally always feeling responsible and engaged, without thinking about it all. The root of such a state exists in our human essence. Such a person sees himself responsible to other human beings, and not to interpretive and conventional values of a thought-constructed self.

Conversely, our usual mode of operation is to be responsible to a self that we know is a mishmash of conflicts. Whoever is in conflict cannot be responsible as there is continuous confusion as to what and to whom or to which aspect of his existence to be responsible to. How can a person whose life does not have a clear direction feel responsible for certain goals, or anything for that matter? Aside from the issue of conflict, one who is captive to factors imposed upon him by external values only feels a sense of duty, not a feeling of true responsibility and engagement.

Our current state of being has us enslaved to our biases, a prisoner of our delusions; therefore we are not free. And the one who is not free cannot be responsible either.

It's important to note that using the word "responsible" in regards to the liberated human being may not be exactly accurate. There are two powerful factors operating within us, namely our "human nature" and the "intellect," which together have the capacity to conduct our existence with authenticity, harmony, and usefulness, without having to put a label on everything and make a big "I" out of it.

**Q:** *In my opinion, if a human is religious then no conflict will be created in him.*

**A:** It's true that there is no conflict in the content of religion, if what you mean by religion is a relationship to the truth—because in truth there is no conflict. In this human being there is neither conflict with the self nor with the world. However, this kind of religiousness is different from our usual religion, which is the ongoing creation of an "I."

# CHAPTER FIVE

# THE COCKEYED SERVANT

I n the previous chapters I described the general structure of thought identity, how it gets created, what attributes it has, and what problems result from it. Now let's see how we can free ourselves from the captivity of this unnatural phenomenon.

We know that thought identity or the "I" resides in memory. For a few seconds, try to not refer to your memory and see if you can have an image of the "I." You certainly cannot! It is your *memory* that confirms your attributes as humble, virtuous, inferior, superior, incapable or capable, brave or timid, etc. Right now, without using your memory, can you tell me who you are? Can you do this?

\*\*\*

**Q:** *Suppose I tell you that I am shy or I cannot defend myself. If you would ask me how I know that, I would have to refer to my memory to answer you. My memory tells me that the other day in a gathering I wanted to say something but I felt too bash-*

*ful to utter a word; or somebody insulted me and I could not even defend myself, therefore I am a bashful or defenseless person. In my opinion it is obvious that without referring to memory we cannot have any image of our "mental identity."*

**A:** Hence, the "I" is the memory storehouse. Therefore if the mind did not have a memory-based activity, meaning the mind did not start its movement from memory, we would not have an image of an "I." We could also describe this in a different way: if the mind does not think about the past tense, the phenomenon called "I" would no longer exist.

Let's see how we can create a situation for the mind that would prevent it from thinking in the past. What I want to say in this context is very simple, but expressing it might require me to be a little crafty. Therefore, please pay close attention.

Every day and night, even in sleep, our *thought* is incessantly busy, wandering and roaming. It travels around the world and comes up with thousands of different imaginary plots. It brings us victory, glory, and greatness. It takes us to fame and ideal circumstances. It ensures us of our uniqueness and provides thousands of other necessities for the "I" to sustain itself and to perpetuate the existence of thought identity in any manner possible.

We usually do not pay attention to thought's roaming and daydreaming. It's as if the mind works automatically, without our involvement, like a mechanical thought-weaving loom. Let us "pay attention" to all this mind-roaming. Up until now, we have not been aware of the activities of the mind and have left it to do all the roaming it desires. *Now, let's bring our awareness and our presence into this roaming process where we can begin to become aware of the mind's activities.*

Suppose someone has asked us to provide a report on our daydreaming. Our assignment is to take notes of any thoughts or imaginings that passes through the mind and report on it. How are we going to prepare such a report? To do so, it's obvious that we need to start *paying attention* and observing our thoughts as they are happening, unlike the way they have been happening unconsciously. This attention can happen in one of two ways. One is that a specific thought comes to mind and exits, and then our memory recalls what we were thinking about a moment earlier. However, our reporting assignment does not accept this method of observation. The thinking-first and paying-attention later is not acceptable in this assignment. The assignment really wants us to pay attention to a thought while it is happening in the mind and not after it is finished. Do you see the difference between these two approaches? For instance, you may think what nonsense this fellow is talking about. At the same moment that you are thinking that thought, pay attention to it; stay aware of thought happening in your mind. Is that clear?

**Q:** *Yes, I understand. I have done this practice before and I know what you mean. This is exactly like having an inner eye behind your physical eye to look at your brain. Gnostics say, "With the same inner eye pay attention to a point in the heart." Now you say, "Pay attention to your thoughts."*

**A:** Yes, both have the same result.

**Q:** *(Another questioner) But I did not get it. Would you explain further?*

87

# THE POWER OF NO THOUGHT

**A:** Please pay close attention. Let's assume that we are watching a movie screen, and we are told some random numbers are going to appear and disappear on the screen in short intervals, and we must read those numbers. How are we going to prepare our minds for this task? It is obvious that our whole attention must stay focused on the screen so we can read the numbers quickly before they disappear. Now let's do the same thing with our thoughts.

The mind is like a movie screen on which thoughts appear and disappear. One thought pops out, runs for some time, finishes, the next thought pops out. These thoughts are like those numbers appearing on the screen. We can pay attention to our thoughts with the same quality of awareness that we did for the numbers. Follow a thought at the moment it gets generated in the brain, pay attention to it by being aware of it, and watch it dissolve and go away. If we do this, we will see that the existence of thought identity is cut off from the root. It is completely obvious why. *The state of "attention" is a mental quality pertaining to the "present."* When the mind gets in the "present" completely, it is no longer roaming around in time because it cannot be in two places at the same time. It cannot be in the present, past, and future simultaneously. In other words, being in the present prevents the mind from accessing memory and retrieving its contents. Our thoughts are usually initiated from memory; and a thought that comes from memory (except for real and physical matters) is in relation to the "I." Or more accurately said: *it is exactly the "I."*

Our memory stores two types of data. One is the real factual information like logic and math, to know two plus two is four;

and the other is about a pitiful person or a dignified person, a successful person or a disappointed person, etc. Now, if the mind didn't have the habit of constantly referring to memory, meaning not *chewing the memory cud*, then there wouldn't be any "pitiful or dignified" and other such dualities, because the mind creates the "I" from the memory.

The question may cross your mind: Well, suppose we could keep the mind in the present and cut its relationship with memory? In that case, would the collection of data referred to as the "I," stored in memory, dissolve and disappear completely? Are you paying attention here?

Let's assume that we could keep our minds in the present for twenty-four hours. Therefore there would be no chance to access memory and bring its contents into the active part of the mind. When twenty-four hours have passed, is thought identity or the "I" in the memory dissolved or just smothered without a pulse for that length of time? Clarifying this problem is very important and is the key to solving a number of problems.

We generally do not have an accurate understanding of thought identity. We think of identity as a "thing," as a reality that exists in us and is a part of our beings. Whereas, the actual content of identity is nothing but thoughts—chewing the cud from the memory repository. Therefore if the mind is kept continuously in check, meaning in the present, the phenomenon of "I" does not get created.

An important point to note is this: "attention" is not a temporary diversion from the norm. The mind is always in attention. We should not consider our current situation as normal.

THE POWER OF NO THOUGHT

All of our current mental activities appear to us as normal and natural. Since our minds are fully accustomed to their everyday situations and their roaming, this does not seem abnormal to us. Presently I am talking to you but all my attention is not with you, meaning I am not relating to you with my whole being. Part of my attention is with you and a big part of it is roaming in other places. While I am looking at you and talking to you, I'm also thinking about whether my talk is interesting for you, whether you are a better talker than me, whether you would criticize me, and hundreds of other thoughts floating in the back of my mind. But a healthy mind, the mind that has not lost its attention to the present, does not rove and roam like that. *The healthy mind always has the quality of "total attention," meaning it is always in one place, completely.*

To summarize, one of the most important factors of the protection and continuity of thought identity is time. If the mind keeps a quality that does not sway in time, then the phenomenon called the "I" will not be created. In order for the mind not to sway in time and not go to memory and the feeding of thought, it must constantly pay complete attention to its activities. *It must be aware of what it is doing.*

Other than becoming aware of the mind's habit of "thinking in time," let's investigate what other factors preserve the continuation of thought identity.

\*\*\*

*Rumi* has a parable in the Masnavi that closely describes our mental situation:

# THE COCKEYED SERVANT

A few hundred years ago, there was an alchemist who had a cockeyed servant (saw double). One day, the master told him to fetch a bottle from the cellar. The servant returned and reported that there were two bottles in the cellar, which one should he bring? The master said, "No, there is only one." The servant went back to the cellar, checked again, returned and said there were two bottles. This time, the master told him to break one of the bottles and bring the remaining one. The servant carried out the master's order, came back and said there was none left.

*** 

From early childhood we have been afflicted with a kind of "dualistic mental view." Our minds have been trained to see a single phenomenon as two. This dualistic view is the most important reason for protection and perpetuation of the mental center we know as the "I." If we feel this dualistic view deeply in ourselves, and become aware that we see a single entity as two, then this awareness causes neither of the "two" entities to remain.

Now let us see what I mean by "dualistic mental view," and how the mind divides a single entity into two.

*We have created a mental center in our memory that we know as the identity or the "I." We know that this center has been built of a collection of attributes* (images that are the results of our interpretations.) *Then we attach some more attributes to this "center."* We say "I" am a distinguished person or "I" am a brave person or other such similar titles. *That means we account for each attribute twice: one that's already in the center, as the center, and one as a newly attached attribute to the center.* Don't forget that the "I" or the center is not a separate entity from each one of the added attributes. This is like the old saying about a man who walks through the forest and can't see the forest for the trees!

Due to the deceptive quality of thought, and a long habit of dualistic views, we do not recognize that there is only the attribute itself, not the "I" plus the attribute. There are only trees, not both trees and the forest. When I say that "I" am incapable, that's exactly like saying "incapable" is "incapable." This is like saying attributes such as humility, fear, sacrifice, self-pity, generosity, and others (all collected in a mental center while the "incapable" attribute is amongst them) are also "incapable." Isn't it that the collection of all those attributes has formed the "I"? Therefore, whether I say "I" am incapable or I say that the other attributes of humility, fear, etc., are "incapable" makes no difference. Does it make any sense to say that the attribute of humility or self-pity is "incapable"?

In fact, thought identity is the result of a mental activity that we call "active thought." This means there is only one specific thinking process with a specific quality at any given time. However, if we break down the result of this process and activity, which is essentially an imaginary activity, we call some of it the "I" and some as the attributes of the "I." These two are constantly in crosstalk and shifting positions with each other. That means that we sometimes consider the attributes *as the "I"* and sometimes the attributes *of the "I."*

To understand this subject better, let us see where and how the "dualistic view" started. Let's assume today is the first day we want to interpret a young boy's behavior. When he does a specific action that denotes kindness, we tell him, "You are a kind kid." The word "kind" gets registered in his mind without it having a clear connection to the specific action. The next day, in relation to another action, we tell him, "You are a generous kid." The word "generous" also gets registered in his mind's repository. The following day when we tell him, "You are a brave kid," and he presumes that the brave attribute is related to the other two attributes ("kind" and "generous"), which by now have become a base or a center in his mind. Later, he will perceive that center as the "I," the collection of things that describe him.

Meanwhile, the third attribute, "brave" which is also registered in his mind, gets added to the other two attributes and they all become a base for the fourth attribute to come. Then the fourth attribute plus the other three attributes become a base for the fifth attribute and so on. Afterwards, when we tell him, "You are a kind kid," he relates this attribute to the other four attributes. That means he takes out the "kind" attribute, which is part of the base, and relates that to *himself* as an attribute separate from the base. The other attributes have the same quality as well. (Note that all these interactions get formed in the child's mind implicitly and over a long period of time.)

Now that we understand there is only one phenomenon at work, we should ask what that phenomenon is. So far, you have been telling yourself: "I" am a "brave" person. That means you have considered two phenomena for yourself: one is the "I" as a "center" and the other one is "brave" as an attribute describing the center. But you just realized these are not two separate entities. The center and its pertaining attributes *are* one and the same entity. Therefore, you should only ask what that *one* entity is. Should we account for the one entity as the "I," or account for it as the attributes of the "I"?

If we consider the *"attributes"* as the entity, the question of what the base of these attributes is, and to whom the attributes belong, will have to be raised. There must be an object of description for an attribute. There should be a flower to which we could ascribe the attribute of beauty. You cannot imagine an attribute without it relating to something. Alternatively, assuming that entity is the "I," the question of what are its attributes will be raised. Can you imagine a center or a mental phenomenon without having an attribute attached to it?

If we contemplate these questions and feel them deeply, *we will see that the mind becomes devoid of identity.* Meaning, neither the "I" nor the attributes of the "I" will remain. That is, the preservation and perpetuation of this imaginary phenomenon is only possible through a dualistic view. As long as we think the "I" is a phenomenon and a pertaining attribute of the "I" is a different phenomenon, they will both continue to exist—albeit, of course, an imaginary existence.

The "dualistic mental view" is one of the mind's strategies to perpetuate thought identity. The mind is continuously busy fabricating an impermanent phenomenon as an identity, using both the base it has created called the "I"; and the attributes it has made up that it then relates to the base. The goal of thought in this plot is to create a "base," as creating a base helps preserve and perpetuate attributes, and due to the attributes the base would be preserved. (Meaning that the survival of the base and the attributes depend on each other. If there is no "I" (or "base") then there are no attributes, and vice versa.)

Whenever we feel this process deeply by becoming aware that thought splits and represents one imaginary thing through two separate avenues, the whole thing disappears. Understanding the dualistic view intuitively, we can begin to sense the bundles of thoughts hanging around in the mind without them attaching to a center (meaning the identification with an "I" that no longer exists.) *This is when the mind goes quiet and senses a spectacular change: "non-existence," meaning being one with the whole existence.* I do not know if I could clarify the subject any further.

***

**Q:** *What you're saying I can feel internally, but I don't really understand conceptually. Could you say more about how the attributes create the "I?"*

**A:** Ok, suppose one hundred people land on an island. In order to manage their affairs, they elect a leader. After electing a leader, do the one hundred people become one hundred and one? Obviously not. The attributes that form our identity are like those one hundred people that always elect one among them as the leader and call him the "I." After this election we may imagine that they have become one hundred and one, a leader and one hundred members. The "leader" is just a borrowed word, a label. Please note that in our example the one hundred residents of the island are for real, but the one hundred "attributes" in our minds are the results of our delusions. In fact one delusive thought out of many thoughts tries to establish a base to protect and manage the other impermanent thoughts. (Or conversely, one hundred attributes form a base.)

Now what would be the result if we became deeply aware that there is no such base, and that this base itself is one of those delusive attributes that thought has fabricated to preserve the other delusions? Try delving into this matter with your whole being.

For instance, say that I once told myself, "I am a pitiful person," and then my thought continuously strived in every way possible to cover for that sense of inadequacy. However, now that I understand that the "I" and its sense of self-pity are both results of interpretation, coming from thought, will my mind again strive to get rid of self-pity? Obviously not.

The mind has realized that the "I" is exactly the same as self-pity and vice versa; and both of these are made up of thought, meaning "active" thought. The "I," self-pity and any other attribute like self-pity, are the same phenomenon. Considering this, what do you think the quality of the mind would become if its workings were clearly exposed? Obviously, it becomes quiet and stops striving. The moment that the mind stops striving and becomes quiet, there is no "I." Because the "I" is the result of the mind's striving to preserve the "I," and the "I" means thought itself.

You may have seen that some animals perceive their tail as something bothersome and separate, and they chase their tail to try and chew it off. The "I" is like the animal and the "attributes" like its tail. The "I" imagines that fear, inadequacy, etc. are separate from itself and therefore it continuously tries to get rid of them. Our difference from animals, in this case, is that an animal's tail is for real and part of its body, but our attributes are the result of chasing around our own thoughts. The whole "thought identity," meaning the "I," is the result of going around itself in a circle. The moment that the mind realizes the "I" and self-pity are one phenomenon, it stops trying to get rid of self-pity, and in that state the mind finds a quiet quality, devoid of any delusions. This means that the mind refrains from trying to think about the future and "becoming something."

A mind that does not think of the future automatically becomes empty of the past. Because for the mind, the mental past is only an issue as long as it thinks of the future and vice versa. In fact, these two are the reverse of each other. When the mind does not think of the future, neither can it think of the past. For instance, the mind clings to an image of self-pity in the memory, then it imagines a future image as "dignity" and constantly thinks about it. If the mind does not think about "dignity," neither can it have an image of self-pity.

Once the mind realizes that the "I" and its attributes are the same phenomenon, it becomes conscious of its own vain and useless striving. Hence, it will stop trying to change anything, hide anything, justify anything, or escape from anything. Afterwards, the mind, as an entirely holistic unit, is conscious and alert, meaning that it finds a "passive" quality, and in a passive state there is no center as the "I" in the mind.

\*\*\*

One other factor in preserving thought identity, as we know, is words and labels. The "I" thought (active thought) and words are the same phenomenon. If we remove the word tag from what we know as "identity," no content will remain. A tree before our eyes is a reality. The word "tree" is just a representative for the actual tree. If you take out the word "tree" from this reality, the reality itself still remains. But if you remove the words from thought identity; nothing is left.

Think about one of the attributes of thought identity and try to feel its content, without having any words entering into your thought. Do this and see what quality the mind finds. Say to yourself, "I am a timid, pitiful, unsuccessful, arrogant, or humble person." Now try to feel timidity, humility, or anything else in yourself without thinking about the words "timid" or "humble." Try to relate to the content of an attribute without involving words. If you do that you can see there is no content to be the subject of thought; and the mind encounters emptiness.

In order not to fall into another thought trap, pay attention to a couple of points. First of all, do not mistake actions and behaviors for the contents of attributes. As we said before, action does not indicate the reality of an attribute. It's correct that "action" is real, but its interpretation as an attribute does not have any reality, other than some interpretive words. Secondly, do not compare your identity with others' or with your past. This means, do not say that since your behavior is similar to some individual's and his/her behavior is pitiful, hence you are also a pitiful person. Or do not say that since you were timid yesterday, you are also timid now. No one says, "Since I was hungry yesterday, I am also hungry today," unless they feel it physically. If you do not think of the word "hungry," you can still feel hunger inside. So in the same manner, try to feel fear and self-pity in yourself, without any words entering into thought.

You can also experience this with feelings such as anxiety, anger, hatred, despair, jealousy, sadness, and the like. These feelings have contents, not just some words. When you experience a feeling of anger, anxiety, pleasure, or sadness, try to feel the content of that feeling without the interference of words, labels, or definitions, in the same way that one can feel a tooth pain without thinking about the word "pain." If you do that, you will see that anxiety, anger, pleasure, and sadness disappear, and a light and blissful state and quality replaces them. The reason for this is that our present feelings have their roots in words. This means that behind every feeling there is a word. As long as thought is preoccupied with thinking about that word, there is a feeling along with it. As soon as thought stops thinking about that word, which is the motive for a specific feeling, that feeling ceases to exist. For example, you call me "stupid" and I immediately become anxious and angry. Anxiety and anger stay with me as long as I think about the word "stupid." If I do not think of the word "stupid," the feeling and the word will both disappear.

Before we get to more questions it is necessary to clarify some marginal points pertaining to our discussion. The points that I have made about how to let go of the "I" are not just limited to those examples. Anyone can find a way in for themselves. However, all ways should lead to a quiet mind empty of thoughts.

Another point to be clear on is that the meaning of the "I," as we use it in our discussions, is different from its usual meaning. Some believe that the phenomenon of "I" is limited to evil instincts, harmful desires, wicked attributes, selfish behaviors and so on. But what we know and talk about here as the "I" is much broader than those notions. To further elucidate, some have used the expression "domineering self." This expression is relatively precise and comprehensive. One of the most important characteristics of thought identity is its commanding and tyrannical quality. Our whole being is enslaved by it and it dictates everything to us.

The other point is that in order to describe a phenomenon that forms our identity we use various expressions during our discussions. Sometimes we may have used or later will use the word "I," "thought identity," "mold," "active thought," "delusive thought," or perhaps other expressions. We need to explain that the meaning and the content of all those words and expressions are the same. The reason for using different expressions for the same phenomenon is that each expression can explain a dimension and a characteristic better than the rest. For example, the word "mold" conveys limitation, confinement, and a feeling of pressure better than other expressions.

*Rumi compares the "mental mold" to walking with tight shoes on a long trail, which is a precise analogy.* This mental mold, first of all limits our share of the infinite existence to only some circumstances that are happening inside the mold. Secondly, the pressure and trouble imposed on us is exactly similar to the feeling of tight shoes on our feet. The expression: *value identity* conveys the fragmented characteristic of an identity that is formed by hundreds of separated thoughts. The expression *thought identity* shows this phenomenon is made of thought, not of spiritual states beyond thought. *Word identity* illustrates the reality that this phenomenon is nothing but some words. So do not be confused by the different expressions. The content of all of them is the same.

The last point is that some presume that the purification of the "I" is only to detach you from materialistic and worldly things. This perception comes from having a limited view of the "I". The problem of the "I" is not materialistic attachments alone. Psychological attachments are considerably broader and much more destructive than materialistic attachments. Basically, it is better to say that the human being is not attached to material things, but rather attached to our interpretations of material things and their face values. In fact, material things are like credits that bankroll psychological values, and that is why human beings are attached to material things.

***

**Q:** *You say that in the state of "attention," the mind becomes empty of the "I." But I have tried this and it does not work.*

**A:** The reason you think it does not work is first of all, the duration of your attention has been too short. The attention should become the predominant quality of the mind. Secondly, at the beginning your attention may not have been complete, but an attention that is mixed with thoughts. It is possible through attention for the upper layers of the brain to become quiet while the lower layers are still preoccupied with the "I" that whispers and chatters away. The longer the attention rests in one place, the deeper it becomes. And the extent of attention getting longer and deeper is proportional to understanding the seriousness of the problem.

In the example of the numbers appearing on a movie screen, there might be a time when they tell you that if you can read the numbers on the screen, you will get a small prize. Another time, they may tell you that if you cannot read the numbers, you will be severely punished. And again, maybe at another time, they will warn you that if you cannot read the numbers, you will be prosecuted. It is natural that in those three cases the degree of attention would be different. In the case of promising a prize, you may not be very serious. Some of your attention may be on the screen but mostly your thought is roaming. However, in the third case your mind finds a different quality. Then your mind's relationship to the rest of the world gets cut off, and your whole being becomes attentive to the movie screen. At that time, with that quality of attention, your mind would not have the slightest movement.

We must feel the graveness of the problem. To demonstrate this, a quote from Rumi may be in order, crying out loudly through the ages:

بازخر ما را از این نفس پلید
کاردش تا استخوان ما رسید

*Buy me back from this sinister tone,*
*Its dagger has arrived at my bone.*

102

Once we realize the aggravation of the problem, the mind becomes totally attentive, such that it stops naturally trying to protect this destructive force, and it becomes quiet and free from suffering.

**Q:** *It seems difficult to imagine an empty mind, a mind that does not have activity or thinking.*

**A:** Yes, since we are accustomed to a fully preoccupied mind, it would be difficult to imagine a quiet and peaceful mind without striving and preoccupation. Our minds have to constantly strive to protect the so-called precious identity. But if we just let thought do its duty, we will see that the mind can become quiet and empty of thought, and that's how it is supposed to be, naturally. The essential quality of a healthy mind is tranquility, and its function only begins at the time there is a real necessity for it to do its job. We use our arms only when we need to do something with them. However, we do not use our thoughts in the same way, which are "the commanders of our beings," and we continuously put ourselves into forced labor and unnecessary self-torture. The reason our minds are incessantly working is that they have to take care of real matters as well as being busy with self-created problems. Now, whenever the mind is not get preoccupied with the "I," we will see that it finds an incredibly quiet quality.

**Q:** *By saying that "thought" is the commander of our being; do you mean that it is the most important phenomenon in the human existence?*

**A:** No, there are some things in human beings that exist beyond thought and cannot even be compared with thought. We cannot describe them as more important or less important, larger or smaller, more valuable or less valuable. Those states that are beyond thought are inherent within us and beyond the domain of thought.

**Q:** *I think when the mind is not active it has a quality similar to just before going to sleep, meaning a state that is tired yet calm.*

**A:** No, It is not a *tired* state. In the state that I am pointing you to, the mind, due to its cells having enough rest, experiences a quality of extraordinary awareness, completely alert. When the body needs to rest, it automatically goes to sleep to revive its energy. In the state without the "I," the human being, physically and mentally, finds a balanced and natural harmony. However, our present state of being is mixed up and inharmonious. On the one hand, due to much unnecessary thought activity, the brain cells are exhausted and in need of serious rest. On the other hand, we override our exhaustion, keep our brain cells active and constantly at work, allowing active thought to take on the role of command center. Without exaggeration we could say that from the time "competitive values" have been formed within us as the "I," we have not been able to sleep and rest in the true meaning of the word. We are always in a state between sleep and awake. Our sleep is always accompanied with anxiety. We are even worrying in sleep about challenges and the instruments with which to overcome those challenges. When we sleep, our minds become a wandering place for the "I" and its desires and hopes, or a screen for parades of unfinished business and struggles.

**Q:** *My question is not directly related to our discussion today. But since it is important to me and not clear, I will bring it* *up. In your book, The Lost Human Being and Self-Knowledge, you have said with great emphasis that study is useless. Whereas I think that to study the works of others helps us gain knowledge and awareness. Why did you make that statement?*

**A:** Undoubtedly, I explained in book that first of all, by study I did not mean "sciences." For you to become a good physician, an engineer or a physicist, it is necessary to learn from others' experiences. This is obvious. Our discussion there was about the subjects of spirituality and morality. So please pay close attention to what I am saying in this regard. Suppose you, as an example, have studied Rumi's *Masnavi.* You have also understood the meaning of his talks. So, the question is: how have you used those talks? Aren't all Rumi's verses, references, and his guidance in regard to reaching the truth, to be used for cleansing the mind from delusions and ideals? Have you reached the truth by studying those references and guidelines? Why haven't you? That is because your mind did not have a learning quality during the studies. You have studied and memorized thousands of subjects, but not with a quality of true learning. If your mind had this real quality of learning, it could have reached the truth by studying a few references or even one. Suppose you read this verse from Rumi:

پیش چشمت داشتی شیشه کبود
ز ان کبودت جمله عالم می نمود

*Gloomy glass before your eye you hold,*
*The whole world is gloomy you told.*

Now, please tell me how you have used this reference. If your mind had the intention and quality of true learning, this single reference alone would have been sufficient to free you from all your confusion and inner darkness. And if the mind does not have such a quality, thousands of such references would be of no use. This verse, "Gloomy glass before your eye you hold," would simply be a theory, an ideology.

Well, now I ask you if, in your opinion, this theory is right, what would be your answer? If you say that it is right, I ask you, how would you know that it is right? Do you see and feel the existence of those dark glasses covering your mind? If you say that the theory is wrong, again I ask you how you know that it is wrong. Have you gained access to your inner being and searched for those dark glasses and found that there are no dark inner glasses? If you have delved into your inner world, Rumi's reference would no longer be a theory but the truth that you have directly perceived with the help of Rumi's reference.

If you have not perceived and felt the truth for yourself (whether there are mental glasses or not), what would be the use of this theory? You have already stored thousands of such theories in your memory without actually feeling their contents directly within yourself. *If your mind was after the truth, it would not be necessary to memorize this much theory, and the help of only one reference would be enough to reveal the truth.* It is not necessary to hear such references from a philosopher or a wise person. Life is full of signs and references; one needs only to open one's eyes and see them.

To study with the kind of quality that we ordinarily do is not only useless, but also it turns us into second hand human beings, snobs, and scholars. Because the "center" doing the studying is an illusion, and illusion is exactly what makes up the "I." Therefore, whatever is gained through that center only makes the "I" heavier. The "I" is like a collection of different embellishments that decorate the human being.

**Q:** *In my opinion, knowing the opinion of others is better than not knowing them.*

**A:** You are not paying attention to my point. Our problem is not in not knowing, but rather in knowing erroneously. Our ignorance and lack of awareness are not due to things that we do not know, they are due to the things we think we know that are actually erroneous. This erroneous knowledge is there because the means of our so-called "knowing" are delusive thought processes. My point is that if our knowledge has been gained through the "mold," not only is it not knowledge and does not help with awareness, but it actually inflates our state of ignorance. The "mold" is equivalent to delusion, and whatever is gained through delusion has the same essence as the delusion.

# CHAPTER SIX

# THORN UNDER THE
# DONKEY'S TAIL

There are many methods and systems touted to help us discover ourselves and confront the "I." But in practice, for many they have become the means for self-deception and distraction. In this chapter, I will briefly review some of these methods.

To begin with, I should mention that the purpose of discussing such methods and systems is to learn about their incorrect characterization of self-realization, not to discuss the specifics of each system or ideology. This means that we want to examine under what conditions the quest for self-realization leads one down the path of self-deceit. Secondly, whatever I say about such methods would apply to any ideology or system of a similar misdirected approach that hinders correct awareness of the truth.

The rationale for my choice of certain ideologies is that I am somewhat familiar with them, and I have experienced their futility in practice. One of these systems is auto-conditioning. The next one is psychoanalysis. We want to know if these systems really help people or are they just a means of consolation. In order to deal with this subject, I will first lay out the general problem. We should define what our real problems are as human beings, as well as their substance and characteristics. Obviously, if we do not identify the problem, we cannot apply the correct solution.

On a broad level we have two kinds of problems. One kind is real and genuine; the other is what we consider as real, yet it is not. Both types of problems have been viewed as such from our particular identity structures and are the direct or indirect results of what I have referred to as "active thought." This type of thought has cut us off from our authentic spiritual nature; namely, from our experience of the state of love. It separates us from unity, it blinds us from a fresh view of life, it wastes our energies in the service of delusive and airy matters, and does not serve our true beings. This type of thought restricts our views by creating walls in our minds. It causes us to accept a limited and singular meaning for our lives, a meaning that does not go beyond the limits of its "mold," causing us to relate to a shadow of life rather than having a direct experience of life.

These are serious problems. Unfortunately, we either do not pay much attention to them, or we are unaware of their existence. Mistakenly, we consider a series of issues that are not the real problems, yet our minds interpret them as such. For example, experiences such as self-pity, shame, inadequacy, or something similar do not truly exist. It is thought identity that interprets one action as dignified and another as pitiful, one action as incapable and another as capable, one action as courageous and another as weak. These are not actual problems, but they are seen as problems within the framework of thought identity. And since the basis of this identity is illusory, the results of whatever is in its domain and its interpretations are also illusory, meaning not real.

Suppose a foreign army has invaded and conquered your land. This army's soldiers have created two kinds of problems. One is that they have captured you, taken away your freedom, harassed you and interfered with your life. Another is that they have conflicts and struggles among themselves that also interfere with your life. Active thought has the same role as these soldiers. It creates problems for you that are targeted at your authentic spirituality. Also, it creates problems with itself similar to those of soldiers, such as disagreements about how to divide the loot. All the problems of war such as defeat and self-pity are in the framework of thought identity.

Now, let's go back to the subject of auto-conditioning, psychoanalysis, or similar ideologies that deal with problems of human psychology and morality. On which of the two kinds of problems mentioned above, real or imaginary, do these modalities focus their attention? What is their agenda? Do they want to rekindle the love that is hidden within us? Do they want to bring us back to our authenticity? Do they want to create unity in our fragmented and compartmentalized beings? Do they want to get rid of the deep ignorance resulting from an identity that is based on delusion? Do they want to change our "old" views to "new" views? Or, do they want to dissolve our shame, pity, and inadequacy?

Do these ideologies want to free our beings from the attack and rule of foreign soldiers, or do they want to get rid of the soldiers' problems? These subjects are what we want to get clear on.

First, let us see what auto-conditioning or self-training might have to say about it. You might be familiar with the famous Pavlov's dog experiment. If not, read about it when you have time. The psychologists used this experiment to try and solve our psychological and spiritual problems. Their theory was that social conditioning had ingrained certain images in our psyches that influence our present day behaviors and actions. For example, the reason I have adopted a stance of self-pity is because I have an image of a pitiful person imprinted within my mind. Now, if possible, by the methods of "reframing" and "autosuggestion," some of the tools and branches of this system, remove the image of a damaged self from my memory and replace it with an image of a dignified, capable, and clever person, and then my actual behavior will follow and become that of someone distinguished and proud.

Let us see how much of this method is accurate or inaccurate, and whether this approach is an essential solution or just patchwork.

"Conditioning" means that our social mores have caused images to become registered in our minds through infusion and repetition, and now we live and act according to those images; meaning that our actions are responses to those images. So far, this is correct. Some images instilled in our minds have formed a mental mold, and now any action we take would be influenced and commandeered by that mold. Being conditioned means that our actions and behaviors are dependent upon whatever the mold dictates to us.

So far, this theory is accurate. First, we have become "conditioned," and secondly, through auto-suggestion, we can create changes in the mold that we think will be desirable and suitable, and we can basically re-condition ourselves. We believe that whatever society has imposed on our minds has been without our choice, will, or awareness, and now we are going to break the old mold through choice and awareness and make a new mold.

However, in this reasoning, there are some subtle points or questions that should be clarified. The first question is who or what factors decide that a certain image is undesirable and what different image should replace it that is desirable? What is the factor that decides that some corners of the mold, or even the entire mold, should change? Isn't this factor the mold itself? We know that our minds have two kinds of activities: one that is active or interpretive and the other passive (objective). In the passive quality, the mind sees everything *as it is*, without any interpretation. In passive thought, the mind sees not talking or being quiet as not embarrassing. But the active thought demands that not talking in a social gathering is an embarrassing character trait.

Well, now I want to assess the mold in order to remake it. What is my means of assessment? It is certainly thought. There's no doubt about that. So let's ask ourselves this question: During our assessment of the mold, which one of these two qualities does the mind have? Is it a passive quality or an active one? It is certainly the active quality, because we said in the passive quality, the mind does not interpret things, everything is what it is, there is no self-pity or its opposite, and there is no value or lack of value. Therefore, during its assessment, the mind's quality is active when it determines, "I do not like this image, and I should change it to another image." Any active movement of the mind means movement within the framework of the mold. Or to put it more precisely, the mind's active movement is *exactly* the mold. The mold or the "I" is nothing but the mind's *interpretive* activity.

How does this work? First of all, the interpretation or assessment is done by the mold itself. Therefore, how do we know if the images that the mold determines as "desirable" or "undesirable" and wants to change are really desirable or undesirable? Isn't the mold imposed upon our minds without our conscious will in the first place? Therefore, every movement of the mind, including its assessment, also has a blind and unconscious quality. The significance of this reality is that anything we discern to be desirable or undesirable does not necessarily have those qualities, it's only an interpretation of our specific mold structure.

Secondly, let us give some credit to the system of auto-conditioning and assume that whatever is discerned by the mind to be desirable or undesirable is valid, and we actually can remove undesirable images from our mold identities and replace them with desirable images. Even so, the real problem is altogether different. The real problem is that the mold itself is basically a foreign entity in our existence, a thinking polyp that must be removed from the root. Our essential work here must be the negation of our fascination with the mold, not the restoration or patching of the same (though patches may be magnificent and have value).

114

Once I become dissatisfied with images of myself as shy or self-pitying, and I want to change them to their opposites, it's as if I prefer one of the mentioned soldiers over another one. If we go one step further and look more carefully, we can see that even the same entity that says "I don't like this soldier but I like the other one" is another one of the soldiers with a destructive quality.

The "new-conditioning of self," even within the framework of the mold, is an inharmonious interaction; and it makes the mold even more artificial and disconnected from the true self than it already is.

As we can see, within the structure of the mold is an unhealthy and continuous cause-and-effect relationship, and every corner of the mold is connected to the whole structure. Therefore, any new image that enters the mind through the methods of reframing, behavioral conditioning or autosuggestion is an incongruent and disconnected image within the whole mold. Additionally, the new image cannot completely erase the previous opposite image, because every image in the whole mold structure is connected with each other and has hidden roots. The only result that can be gained by replacing one image with another is that it mixes up the mold identity's relative balance and contributes even more artificiality to human behavior than was present in the first place. I have clearly seen this in many individuals who have used these types of systems. Their behaviors and actions have taken on the qualities of imitation and parroting.

The same problems exist in psychoanalysis. In short, psychoanalysis ascertains that human behavior is influenced by unconscious motives. Psychoanalysts claim that by analyzing behaviors and correlating them with each other, they can convert unnatural and aberrant behaviors to normal behaviors. They also say that the hidden causes of our present behavior can be found in the factors that influenced our personalities during childhood. This is the essence of psychoanalysis and the rest is details and derivatives of the same.

I said that every mind-movement that has an active quality indicates that the mind is thinking about the foreign army soldiers and their problems; therefore the more mind activity, the more it feeds the problem and adds additional complexity. But now that we understand that our internal "soldiers" are nothing more than the activity of the mind, if we try to resolve the problem with further mental interpretation, then it is exactly like trying to extinguish a fire with gasoline. In this context, Rumi has given us a very precise hint:

کس بزیر دم خر خاری نهد
خر نداند دفع آن بر می جهد
برجهد آن خار محکم تر زند
عاقلی باید که خارش بر کند

*A nasty thorn lands in the donkey's tail,*
*The higher he jumps that sore may curtail.*

*With every jump the thorn digs deeper without fail,*
*A wise man is to pull the thorn, from Kiang's tail.*

Striving to resolve a problem through interpretive thought is exactly like the donkey's jumping and hitting the thorn deeper in the body. And in psychoanalysis, for obvious reasons, there is a high degree of mental interpretation.

Let's look again in a very simple and clear manner at how psychoanalysis works:

My problem is that I am very sensitive and short-tempered, and I feel extremely resentful if anyone ignores me in any way. So I consult with a psychologist. Or maybe my problem is that I am shy or feel pitiful. Then the psychologist starts asking questions about my situation in my childhood, my family, my upbringing and schooling, my financial situation, the people who had major roles in my upbringing, and questions that might help explain to him, and eventually to me, what factors in childhood are the causes of my present problems.

If you pay close attention, you will see some of the obvious fundamental characteristics of active thought, which are based on delusion. First, there is the interpretive characteristic. From the moment I consult with a psychologist and I bring up shyness, self-pity, fear, inadequacy, or any such problem, my mind is already preoccupied with delusive interpretations. More precisely, I have brought a "self-made" problem to the psychologist, not a real problem. The psychologist, who accepts my problems as problems and tries to get to their roots through analysis, has effectively partnered in my "delusive thinking." Meaning, the psychologist and I are collaborating to resolve a bubble, not a real problem.

In analysis, in addition to using labels, the mind becomes busy roaming around in the past to find causes for problems. And we know that any movement of mind in time can only exacerbate a psychological problem. The mind's motion in the past or the future is like gasoline added to the fire of thought identity or delusive identity. And we know that at the heart of the problem is the identity itself.

The only useful help that a psychologist or equivalent can provide me is the understanding of the reality that "You do not have an illness except that you think you are ill." Is it anything other than this? If I consider myself to be self-pitying, inadequate, defective in some way, or any other problem, is it a really true, or is it simply a mental interpretation, a self-created problem of the mind?

*** 

From the content above, some implicit conclusions can be made that are more important to pay attention to than the actual psychotherapeutic system being employed. One of these conclusions, in regard to psychological matters, is that any improvement, correction, or progress that is made gradually in time is meaningless. *The reformation and the change must happen all at once.* This means that whatever delusions are nested within the mind (and we now know them to be the "I") must be removed from the mind all at once rather than gradually in time. To think "I will be better tomorrow or next year" is a deception imposed on us by thought to guarantee its survival from today to tomorrow and from tomorrow to thousands of other tomorrows, and it does its best to keep us unaware of the essential possibility of letting go of the "I" all at once. (Please remember that our discussion is about thought identity, not our true spiritual nature.)

Now let's see what gradual improvement means in regards to thought identity. We can imagine a few possibilities here. One possibility is that we actually want to preserve and improve the thought identity. For reasons that should be clear by now, any attempt to preserve or improve upon the thought mold of the "I" doesn't make a lot of sense. This phenomenon is foreign in our being and should be uprooted. *When it comes to spirituality, mental activity is only an interference.* Active thought is not an appropriate partner for spirituality. Therefore, we should decidedly prevent this intrusion upon our spirituality and not try to "correct" it or improve upon it. If you wanted to hear or see better would you try to fix your hand? I hope all of us are starting to comprehend this truth from the depths of our beings and stop falling for the mischievousness and the deceit of our thoughts.

Now, back to the question of whether the annihilation of the delusive "I" phenomenon should happen all at once or gradually.

To answer this question, once again we should consider the characteristics of thought identity. Inherent in the structure of this phenomenon are some principle stems and some branches. The principle stems are based on values that have been presented to us and get registered in our minds from childhood. For example, you should be smarter than others, you should know everything, you should be clever, brave and capable, you should be able to handle any job, you should be likeable, you should not need anything from others, you should be invincible, and whatever else that has become a value in our society.

Then, some branches have grown from these stems. For example, jealousy, hatred, sensitivity, self-pity, fear, despair, failure, blame, conflict, and many other problems are dependent on principle values and the inevitable results of values.

Now let's see what the topic of improvement and "gradually-becoming-better" means in regard to the structure of such labels and their characteristics. It seems obvious that we cannot do anything about the branches or the byproduct problems. Feelings of jealousy, self-pity, fear, anxiety, or ignorance cannot stand independently on their own; they are the byproducts of other problems. As long as I need to be smarter, more vital, and better looking than you, I will inevitably, in relation to you, have feelings of fear and anxiety, jealousy, sensitivity and vulnerability, malignancy and hatred, a pretentious life, and a host of other problems. However, I cannot do anything with these byproduct problems as long as the underlying values exist.

So, what we are left with is values. Is the letting go of the values that form the "I" a gradual matter, or should it happen all at once? If we imagine that the gradual letting go of values is possible, then that notion itself is coming from an incorrect view of the essence of the phenomenon of "I." The reason that human beings throughout history have not been able to overcome this destructive phenomenon is due to a lack of knowledge of its characteristics and essence. We imagine thought identity as an object separate from thought, and all our attention is towards this object rather than thought itself. We look at the "I" but not at its creator, which is thought. And this mistake is the reason for the survival and continuation of the phenomenon of "I" and all its related problems. We ask how we can get rid of the "I," while all the time we are unaware that in truth there is no "I." The "I" does not in reality exist, except in thought. The nature of our error is mental. And resolving this mental error is what's of the essence here, not "getting rid of" it.

Let's assume that there is a defect in my system of thinking, and due to that problem, I imagine there are ghosts in this room. In this case, is my problem to get rid of the ghosts or is it to resolve the misperception in my thinking? Are you paying attention to this point? *The essential reason we are continuously defeated in our struggle with the "I" is that we think about ghosts, not about resolving our defective thinking.* And any perception of the possibility of letting go of the "I" in time is also derived from a clouded view.

As long as we think about the "I" and its "values" as an entity separate from thought, meaning "ghosts," the possibility of "gradual letting go" is also entertained. But if our attention is on resolving our errant thinking, we would see that correction, evolution, improvement, and gradual letting go do not have any real meaning. They are simply excuses and tricks of the mind to perpetuate the survival of the "I" by the "I."

Another reason we entertain this idea of evolution and gradual improvement is that not only do we perceive the "I" as reality, we perceive the attributes that form the "I" to be real as well. The truth is that these attributes are merely *shadows* of reality created by our minds. By understanding that what we believe to be reality is actually a delusion, we can also begin to see that any idea of gradual improvement is delusion as well.

Please pay close attention to what I mean by this: I might know a foreign language, have a fancy house, and own a very expensive car. These are three different subjects, and the phenomenon of "I" is not constructed from the foreign language plus the house plus the car, but the face *value* that I perceive in them. Therefore, though the subject consists of three different things, what I feel is the "value" of these combined collective credits. The subjects of the value are various, but my mind only ascertains an absolute value. Rumi's point in the following verse conveys this meaning:

گر هزارانند یک تن بیش نیست
جز خیالات عدد اندیش نیست

*Thousands, though one body and naught,*
*Nothing but number-thinking thought.*

Finally, we have arrived at the question, should the eradication of this absolute value be gradual or all at once?

Please pay close attention to the answer: it is correct that the "I" is basically imposed on our minds by external factors and registered in our memories; but at this moment that you and I are talking, nobody except us is responsible for the preservation and continuation of that identity. Therefore, if we deeply and honestly want to have this entity out of our minds, it could happen all at once.

Since childhood this entity has been considered necessary and precious and, has been imposed on our minds, and we have been so preoccupied with it that we never doubted its authenticity. Due to our ignorance of the true nature of self, to our fragmented views, and our deceptive thinking patterns, we have never noticed that all our problems and suffering are coming from this entity. Since we are unaware of this truth, we remain firmly attached to this entity. Now, if we realize the aggravation of this precious thing and honestly want to be free of it, we can cut its life at once. It is only we ourselves who perpetuate the life of this entity by dragging it from today to tomorrow and tomorrow to future tomorrows.

If our minds did not continue to weave thought and imagination together to preserve this imaginary entity, it would no longer exist. If I fully realized the aggravation of this imaginary entity that my own thought has created, and which I honestly no longer want to exist, then why doesn't my mind stop its delusive thinking once and for all? Does it make any sense for the mind to continue to create a delusive phenomenon and then hope to be rid of it over time?

If I have realized the aggravation of thought identity, why not be done with it here and now? Why do I procrastinate? Thinking "later today" or "maybe tomorrow" is how thought deceives us for the continuation of the "I." Thought says, "Let's deal with this phenomenon today, and either it gets better or we can get rid of it tomorrow." But alas, thousands of tomorrows come and go and this thing does not change.

We should be aware that if the mind were honest in its intention to be rid of thought identity; it could cut off its life in an instant. Or to put it more accurately, the moment that thought *honestly* wants to be rid of itself, then it no longer exists, since it is only thought that creates and perpetuates its life.

*On the path of consciousness and liberation, pay attention to a fundamental principle that can aid in avoiding much deceit and erroneous thinking: Do not think about ghosts, meaning the "self" or the "I." Rather, put your whole attention on the quality of the movement of your thoughts. Whenever you concern your-self with the existence of an "I," you are implicitly assuming that the "I" is a reality. And as long as your mind assumes it to be a reality, its continuation is guaranteed. The moment the mind stops thinking about an "I" and watches its own movements, the "I" automatically disappears.*

\*\*\*

Based on our discussion, another implicit observation can be derived that all people who live from the mold of thought identity, from the psychological perspective and its general characteristics, are the same. The differences we see in individuals are simply differences in the types of molds and their particular actions and strivings to preserve it.

For example, one of the mold characteristics is ignorance. Thought mold keeps the mind surrounded and preoccupied within a narrow confine, and the subject of all its preoccupation is itself a delusion and not reality. This means all "mold-beings" are living in a state of slumber while awake, immersed in total ignorance and a deep lack of awareness. And from this perspective, they are all the same.

It is necessary to mention a few additional points about the idea of gradual improvement and the differences in human beings. You may ask the question, how can we say that there is no difference between someone who's been on the path of Gnosticism or psychology or any other system for the past twenty years, someone who is working on him or herself and the purification of the "I," and someone who has just started? We could say that in one way, they are similar and in another they are different. The difference between someone who started twenty years ago and the one who has just begun is that the first one has possibly realized intellectually that they are a slave to the "I," and thus feel the desire to be liberated from such more than the other who just started.

Let's imagine that a few of us are moving to a city. As long as none of us has reached the city, we have no news of the city because we have yet to reach it, and there is no difference between us. However, from another view, you might be just a few steps away from the city and someone else a hundred steps away and another person one thousand steps away, and so there are slight differences among us. The city is that unknown state beyond thought that we are all moving toward and yet are still unaware of. Either it has been revealed to us or it hasn't.

Now imagine that there is a midway between that state and the "thought mold," what would be your excuse for keeping and justifying the mold. Any excuse would be a positioning of yourself somewhere on the scale of improvement in order to stay ignorant and postpone your essential arrival there.

*If you have studied Rumi's Masnavi carefully, you might have clearly seen the same meaning conveyed. Rumi has not pointed to any scale of how strong or weak the "I" might be. He says, "Dualistic views get diminished little by little," but he does not say that the "I" itself becomes weaker little by little. Everywhere he sees the "I" as synonymous to the devil, and as such, there are no semi-devils. He also sees pure being, devoid of the "I," has a divine, clear, angelic quality. And he sees the transition from that state (thought mold) to this state (beyond thought) as a complete dying of the "I," as nonexistence, as no self what-soever, not as a weakening of the "I."*

Before we end today's discussion it's necessary to clarify two marginal points. The first point is that when it comes to thought identity, humans are not principally different from one another. We are not to be concerned with the character, state, and quality of another's psyche. Our work is on ourselves, not the collective. Our goal is to know our own self, not others. The second point is that whenever during our discussion we mention a verse from Rumi, or we include his point of view on certain observations, our intention is to receive help from a clear, beautiful, and literary *transmission* of truth. We are not looking to see if Rumi concurs with our opinion about a problem, so that we will then know the problem is exactly the way we say it is. I do not bring Rumi's opinion as a proof and a testament, even if he or somebody else has clearly seen and described the truth. We should simply consider his references as guidelines for our own self-investigation. We should receive their support, while attempting to discover the truth directly for ourselves. We must not adopt the subordinate position that since Rumi has said it then it must be the truth.

\*\*\*

**Q:** *Considering that you are talking about human beings in general and not any specific individual or society, accepting the idea that individuals from various societies are not different from each other is difficult and seems far from the reality. Individuals from different cultures have fundamental differences.*

**A:** I am saying that the basic principle of "thought identity" does not differ from one human being to another. Supposedly the people of Germany are different from the people of Iran. The German traditions are different from the Iranians'. Their way of living, their relationships, their laws, and many other things are different, but I do not view those things as fundamental principles of our shared human experience. I know that lack of love in the true sense is a principle. I know that living in our thoughts rather than the present moment is a principle. I know that feeling alienated from the self is a principle. And I know the gravity of our existence as human beings who are molded by thought identity and external factors that keep us running with quality of "propaganda-ism." It also means that as molded humans we consist of a bunch of propaganda.

What you are referring to are the different types of propaganda and how they create different molds, but what I am pointing to is the essence of propaganda and how in general it changes us into aimless, compulsive, and unconscious beings, without a sense of discernment. When we are under the influence of propaganda, we live our lives second hand, meaning that we relate to life and circumstances according to the opinions of others and do not experience life directly, clearly, or freely.

When you observe the lives and the relations of German people, it may seem to you that the quality of their lives is much better than yours. People there do not interfere with each other, and they do not cause trouble for each other. They follow the law, and the kind of violence that exists here does not exist there. They enjoy greater social and political freedom, together with many other differences. But we have also seen many nations that act responsibly and enjoy a great level of freedom leave themselves blindly in the hands of a few, and all at once with a little propaganda they go off destroying any discipline, law, culture, and civilization. Any responsible human being who is not conscious and free within themselves is prone to this.

As molded human beings, we do not act based on consciousness and inner freedom, unaffected by the contamination of propaganda. Our behaviors have a blind quality. This is what I mean by a fundamental human principle. Of course, there are some minor, apparent, and delightful differences in the boundaries of these principles. From a broader and deeper perspective, we do not have a sense of true responsibility except in trivial matters such as job responsibility, family responsibility, national responsibility, and as such, we see ourselves as responsible. From these so-called responsibilities, destruction arises. An American feels responsible to another American but unfriendly toward a Russian. A Russian is the same way towards an American. Arabs vs. many others, Whites vs. Blacks, this nation vs. that nation, this family vs. that family; we all have such relationships. And the "I" is at the center of all these prejudices that divide us.

**Q:** *So are you saying that all human beings are the same in regard to ignorance and consciousness?*

**A:** Yes. What normally seems to us as different is in the context of knowledge and science. You may know things that I do not know; therefore your knowledge is more than mine. However, what I mean by "ignorance" and "consciousness" is more in the realm of spirituality and the ignorance of our true nature. A mind that looks at life through the "mold" is essentially ignorant.

The mold keeps our minds in confinement and darkness, meaning that we relate to each other superficially.

Let's assume that I have never ventured out of the village where I was born, therefore I imagine the world is bound to where I live. You, however, have seen the adjacent village beside your own village, and you imagine the world is bound to these two villages. Another person, in addition to these two villages, has seen a city, and he or she imagines the world to consist of these two villages plus a city. All three of us from a principle point of view are the same; that is, all three imagine the world to be within the boundaries of where we live. But we differ from each other from the standpoint that the world is limited to a village for me, two villages for you, and two villages and a city for the third person. Our mental boundaries are our molds. How big or how small the mold does not matter; it's the mold itself that matters.

**Q:** *Reaching the spiritual state you are describing is extremely difficult and could even be said to be impossible, especially if you are suggesting we reach that state all at once. Isn't it the usual experience for a human being to get confronted with a depressing dead end in regards to what you are talking about? Yes, we have somehow deceived ourselves, and we have kept ourselves busy with things that we thought were right. Perhaps we feel living with the "I" is aggravating, yet on the other hand letting go of it is very difficult.*

**A:** First of all, letting go of the "I" is not difficult; however it *is* scary. Secondly, what exactly are you referring to that gets the human being into a depressing dead end? If you have seen deeply that the "I" you have called yourself is a foreign phenomenon, then you should begin to feel freer and more comfortable than before.

Suppose somebody insults you, and then you immediately feel sad, disappointed, and inferior. Now, if you understand that the insult is pointed at a foreign entity in your being and not your true self, do you still feel inferior, disappointed, and sad?

Let's say, you tell me that what I talk about is nonsense, and I feel uncomfortable because of your comment. The next moment you tell me that what I talk about is good and makes sense to you, and I feel happy. Therefore, like a flattered beggar I would look to see what kind of judgment you might make about me next, and what you might take away from or add to my identity.

Now, if I realize that neither your insult nor your praise has a correct basis (because they are formed by your own mental criteria) and that your insult and your praise are pointed at a delusive "I," meaning pointed at a being that does not have authenticity and is an abusive phenomenon, then wouldn't I feel more comfortable? Wouldn't my fear, anxiety, and dependency, and many other problems as well, disappear in relation to you?

**Q:** *This is like someone who slaps the invading soldiers or gives them sweets. It is obvious that soldiers have no true relationship with me; they are only occupying my country. Therefore, why should I have any concern, interest, or sensitivity towards their happiness or unhappiness?*

**A:** That is completely correct. Both the insult and the praise are directed at the soldiers, only in my own home. As we continue investigating these matters deeper and deeper, we become aware of this truth that even the phenomenon that gets hurt from the insult or gets happy from the praise is part of the soldiers as well.

Do you remember the subject of emotions? We said that any feeling that is a reaction to thought is serving thought identity and is superficial and does not have depth and intensity. Any joy or sorrow whose source is based on thought values is not deep. Doesn't the awareness of these truths cause us to not want to spend our whole lives and all our energies catering to such an artificial phenomenon?

Despite all this, you are suggesting that you are filled with delight anyway; but if you scrutinize this belief you can see that so far you have been more unhappy than happy. The accumulation of our not-delightful moments, our fears, our self-pity, our depression, and our undesirable feelings begins to outweigh their opposites.

**Q:** *I always have a fear if I lose the "I," my mental predicament might become even worse than it is presently. Meaning, by losing the "I," I become nothing.*

**A:** A store owner gave two jars of vinegar to one of his clientele to taste and to see which one was the sourest. The man tasted one of the two and claimed one to be sourer than the other. The vinegar owner asked how he could say that the first one was sourer without tasting the other. The man replied that the one he tasted was so sour he didn't think anything could be sourer.

The story of thought identity and our current situation is like this. We have yet to taste or experience the unknown experience of no "I," but given how aggravating and sour our present lives are, I do not think there could be any situation sourer than this.

However, you are saying that in surrendering to this state, it is possible you might become nothing and that this nothing is something fearful. *Whereas, the truth is, the whole mystery of existence and the meaning of life is in this state of "being nothing."* Everything is in this state, without being able to objectify this state as a thing or being able to describe it.

However, it is very important that you not try to think about this state or to seek it. Just look at what you are, without imagining what you are not. Just investigate the fear without reaching for courage. As long as you are thinking about courage you will not get it, because any imagination that you might have about courage is the product of thought, and thought cannot know the content of an unknown quality. *Any spiritual state that is described by thought is like mirage.* The root of the mirage is thought, as if we imagine we have seen water then it will be so. And no matter how far we follow that thought with our imaginations, we will never reach it. Such water will remain forever out of our reach. As we move forward, not even one step is reduced from the number of steps needed to reach infinity.

Whenever we seek for something psychologically, in every psychological goal and hope, inevitably we are projecting something into the future, and time plays exactly the same role as the infinite amount of steps between the water and ourselves. The only way to freedom over the wall of thought that has been woven around our minds is by looking at the wall itself, without thinking of what might be on the other side of the wall. Because no matter what we imagine is on the other side of that wall, it has basically the same substance and color of the wall itself. I hope that you can understand this essential point. The only wall that

132

lies between freedom and you is the wall of thought, and any movement of thought activity to get beyond the wall only reinforces the wall.

**Q:** *If not through thought, then how can we free ourselves from the wall? You say that thought is not a proper means for solving psychological problems; so then what should we do?*

**A:** If you are paying close attention to what I am saying, the answer is obvious. Thought has two activities. One is passive, the other active. The realization of the truth that *any* active movement of thought only causes more trouble should be enough for the mind to switch to the passive state. And this would be the end of the problem.

# CHAPTER SEVEN

## DO WE SECRETLY ENJOY
## DISAGREEMENTS?

W hen I meet with people publically to discuss the matters that are the subject of this book, I sometimes run into certain hindrances to a useful and logical discussion. As humans, what is gravely needed at this time in our evolution is to develop ways of communicating that avoid arguments and promote cooperative exchange. Therefore I would like to clarify some of the most common and essential problems that can get in the way of cooperative exchange in regards to speaking, listening, responding, and giving feedback.

First let's consider what the purpose of a discussion is. Why is it that you and I get engaged in a discussion? First there must be a topic of discussion, and that topic can sometimes be a point of contention or misunderstanding. Considering this, what should be our relationship in this engagement? It is obvious that it should be a cooperative one. Would anything other than this be truly beneficial? If we encounter an unknown phenomenon, for instance a plant, a philosophical system, or a subject of moral debate, and we get interested in examining that phenomenon so that its essence becomes clear to us, what should be our mindset? Should we confront each other from the beginning and insist that we are right and the other party is wrong? Obviously not. If we start our work with such an intention, the discussion does not have any opportunity to proceed.

Whenever we examine a subject, we assume that at least a portion of that subject is unknown and unclear to us, so with each other's help, we want to clarify and remove any ambiguity. Now, if from the beginning of our discussion, I say that I am right about the subject and you are wrong, and you say the same, this would mean the subject is already clear to both of us, in which case what exactly do we need to discuss?

Discussion in the truest sense is the cooperation of individuals in order to clarify a subject that has ambiguous and unclear points. However, sadly, this is not usually the case between humans. Often there is no quality of cooperation and no desire to clarify; rather we use discussions as an excuse and a battleground for antagonism and one-upmanship.

Now let us see what causes this. Let us investigate why instead of cooperation, we often consider each other rivals and our discussions so often take on defensive, negative, and destructive qualities.

We know that all our relations are influenced by thought identity, its needs and its characteristics. In principle, our communications with each other are channeled through this destructive medium. If the apparent and hidden interferences of such a destructive devil were not at work, there would be no dispute and contention. Inherent in thought identity are scores of unpleasant, destructive, and negative characteristics, which when entered into any conversation, the quality of that relation would become unnatural and destructive.

For example, one of the fundamental characteristics of thought identity is that it is empty of anything real. Just from this one characteristic problems can arise that would change our discussion from a useful and constructive one to an open disagreement or dispute.

In a previous chapter I wrote that thought identity is nothing but empty words. Therefore, since thought has woven this empty identity and insists on its preservation, it struggles to compensate for its innate nothingness and give us a kind of quasi feeling that there's some meaningful content there. One of thought's mechanisms for bringing about quasi contents is to intentionally create problems that will challenge itself and bring about some excitement or anxiety within us to keep itself occupied. Perhaps you have noticed that when we as humans encounter a problem, we internally get an exciting, warm and fuzzy feeling. It's like something inside starts cooking and brings some warmth and movement to life. The role of this activity and warmth is to fill the emptiness. We often account for this state of excitement and warmth as a substitute for "spirituality," so that we do not feel our lack of spirituality.

Considering just this one characteristic, we can clearly see that we are not as interested in solving problems as we are in deliberately creating a problem out of any small matter so that we can wrestle with it, hoping to find a resolution and claim our prize. *In fact it seems more psychologically prudent to create, preserve, and engage in problems, than to clarify or remove them.* If a problem is clarified, then there is no problem by which we can challenge ourselves. So, when this inner motivation also enters into our communications with each other, can we expect and hope for cooperation?

Have you noticed how ready we are to make a problem from anything and establish that as the ground for antagonism and argument? Have you noticed how we normally pose a problem to be solved with a rough and contentious quality? We take on this posturing because we secretly enjoy disagreement. We would like for others to reject our opinion so that we can find an excuse to engage in an argument.

For instance, if someone brings to you a point of contention and then defends it, just tell him or her that their opinion is right and you agree with it. You will see how quickly they will soften drop their aggression. It is like piercing an inflated ball and flattening it. More interesting yet, in many cases, the person may change their position about the subject with some seemingly adept logic so that they can again take a side opposite from you, and then wait for you to say an opposing word to jump on.

There are some individuals who create an imaginary opponent and start arguing with it. Many of us when we are alone get engaged in discussion and argument with ourselves or someone else inside our heads. This readiness for argument and contention indicates that creating a problem and then wrestling with it serves a very important psychological role for us.

Possibly you see a political or religious group that is in disagreement with other groups. Then you see that people of each group find disagreements among themselves, which then fragments the group. Later you notice that each branch of the group becomes further divided. All of this indicates that opposition serves as a kind of psychological drug for us. To oppose and entangle ourselves in problems is like fuel for the thought identity engine. To oppose gives us a quasi-psychological liveliness. Therefore, the truth is, basically we're not interested in solving problems. We only want to keep our *identities* alive by means of entertaining ourselves with problems.

When considering problematic subject matter, one of the byproducts of this psychological need is that individuals pay more attention to their own excitement and entertainment than they do to being instrumental in resolving the issue. Look and see. Do the majority of the subjects that we as humans, individually or collectively, keep ourselves busy with have this quality or not? If we are writers we tend to write about a subject that is full of excitement and fuss, rather than to be of any true service.

For example, we might criticize the government and take a revolutionary posture. If we are politicians, we always have an exciting trick up our sleeves. If we are journalists, we push "hot" and violent news, not useful news. A newspaper headline might be: "The last letter from Napoleon to his wife was discovered, and now investigators are engaged to see if the letter is authentic or not." Or this one: "A mace was found that some believe belonged to Rostam (a legendary Persian figure) while others claim that it belonged to Sohrab (another legendary figure)." Then both groups get into a debate to have their opinions prevail. However, neither party bothers asking what would be the use of such a discussion! Suppose it's not possible to know whether Napoleon's letter is authentic or that the mace belonged to either Rostam or Sohrab; then what benefit would we hope to obtain from all these debates? Of course, with the power of logical reasoning, which is one of the properties of thought identity, we could fabricate viability and results to rationalize the subject. For example, we may say if proven that such a big mace belonged to Sohrab, we could conclude that Sohrab could not have been killed by Rostam (Sohrab was Rostam's son who was killed in a highly dramatized father/son fight.) And suppose, we could conclude that outcome, and then what next? We could come up with another point of contention for debate.

In the previous chapters I pointed out that one of the ways that thought uses to escape our inner emptiness is to adopt an ideology and then nurture an attachment to that ideology in order to feel personally identified with it, striving to view our own identity exactly as that ideology. This is another essential matter that changes the quality of discussions from cooperation to conflict and opposition.

For example, maybe you believe in communism, and from that belief you have formed an identity for yourself, and so have I from its opposite. Now, maybe outwardly we begin a discussion or argument about communism, but inwardly, we put our focus on each of our personal identities and try to defend the righteousness of our identities, not communism or its opposite. In this case, could we expect that our discussion will have a cooperative and constructive quality or outcome? Certainly not. From the start our relationship has a confrontational, defensive, and combative quality designed to condemn each other's identity, and what is completely missing is a sincere effort to clarify the problem.

# DO WE SECRETLY ENJOY DISAGREEMENTS?

An offshoot of such an approach is that individuals consider the *magnitude* of a topic more important than its usefulness. Since individuals attach themselves to ideologies and systems and adopt them as their identities, they think that the bigger and the higher level the topic or ideology is that they are talking about, the higher stature they can obtain from the discussion. However, unaware of the fact of how utterly empty and insignificant we people of thought identity are, no matter how big a subject we talk about, we still remain small.

***

In a previous chapter someone brought up a subject that either had philosophical aspects or was not related to our discussion. I wanted to point out that discussing such subjects will not help us, and that our problem is ourselves. As long as we do not resolve this problem, we cannot truly resolve any other problem. The reason is obvious. Our minds are our tools and means for investigation and examination of problems. But these tools presently function sketchily and sporadically. We know that our minds have become a repository for delusions that have manipulated and clouded our minds, and which are our means of examining and referencing everything in life. Therefore we cannot see life's circumstances as clearly as they really are.

Our most important job, before anything else, is to clear up these delusions. As long as we are not yet familiar with all that is happening in this "small bowl" of the brain, and as long as we have not removed the obstructions that exist in our communications, how can we comprehend larger subjects such as the philosophy of being, the meaning and purpose of life, the essence of "to be" and "not to be," and the existence of the truth?!

\*\*\*

Now, let us go back to our discussion and look at things from another perspective. Do you remember that I said there are generally two kinds of problems in life, one is real and the other is mental or self-created? For example, stained teeth and a hungry stomach are real problems. But the stigma of addiction and the image of being poor are the result of our mental interpretations. One of the reasons that any discussion on the topic is futile and potentially destructive is that in most cases, the subject of the discussion is the image we have of what it is to be an addict, not the stained teeth. This means that we often have a discussion about a mental problem, one that is self-created and full of air. Outwardly, we may bring up the stained teeth, but inwardly the image of the addict is the dominant factor in our discussion. And this matter becomes one of the reasons for our disagreement. In rare cases, if the subject of our discussion really is the problem of the stained teeth, the image of the addict interferes with our views and hinders us from seeing the problem as it really is. And, as soon as our mental images interject themselves into the discussion, the conversation already has a slight confrontational and defensive quality.

Our mental images are our identities. We have created identities for ourselves comprised of values and beliefs. Our current situation is that if we want to listen to the opinions of others, without mental images and biases, if we want to examine and confirm their correctness, it is like we have agreed to give up our identities in exchange for the other party's identity. When you are talking, my mold identity perceives your viewpoint as an arrow that wants to pierce that mold. Therefore I hold my mold as a shield against your words with an energy of defensiveness and toughness. This is the reason that we do not listen to each other with open ears and open minds, free of biases.

Because of these factors, thought identity is essentially an unnatural and destructive brew. And unfortunately, we enter into our relationships with this unnatural way of being. This means that basically any communication that thought identity has with the external world is a destructive one. The fibers of its fabric are woven of hatred, anger, fear, the desire to dominate, and scores of other destructive attributes. Therefore, how can we have a useful and constructive relationship by such a destructive means?! Our various values, each of which is a pillar of support for the structure of thought identity, enter into our relationships and further contaminate the mind.

Generally, one of our values is "I need to know everything about any matter." This particular value undermines any possibility of cooperation and encourages a sense of pretense in regard to how much knowledge we have about everything. If we know nothing about the subject, we may divert the conversation to a topic we do know something about, even though it may have nothing to do with the initial subject matter. We might play with words, talk about unnecessary and marginal topics, speak fallacy, and in order to show our extensive knowledge, maybe we string together a few disconnected lines we have memorized from books and interject them into the discussion. In short, we create a thousand problems rather than accept that we do not know something.

Let's consider another value, "We are better than others," which causes us not to be patient listeners. Have you noticed how impatiently we listen to each other? As soon as we figure out what the other party is talking about, and even without understanding the matter, our ears and our mind's relationship to their words is already cut off. In the interim, we spend all our effort fabricating a response we feel we must throw at the talker like an arrow. The reason for this is that the listening position makes us feel weak and disadvantaged. We think that the advantage is with the speaker, and the listener is put into a position of submissiveness. All of us are better at speaking than listening, and we tend to talk more than we listen. This is because we consider ourselves to be our words. Therefore, we think that the more we talk, the more we *are*, the more we *exist*, whereas listening does not attribute such power.

As we enter into our future discussions, may they have a cooperative and constructive quality. May our dialogues be without grudge or aggression. Let us be aware that everything we talk about comes from the mold and it is dictated by the mold. Everything that we hear goes through our molds and then gets to our minds. Let's be aware that our communications, our sense of logic, our examinations, philosophies, life goals, and everything else are influenced and determined by the mold. And the mold is not a thing that has been selected by our conscious discernment. *We look at life circumstances through the criteria imposed on our minds by others; hence, we cannot trust the accuracy of their evaluations.*

# DO WE SECRETLY ENJOY DISAGREEMENTS?

*** 

**Q:** *You are saying that everything we do, including our communications, is influenced by the "mold." So, by becoming aware of this reality, is awareness enough to neutralize the effect of the mold? I mean, we have the mold anyway, so what does it matter whether we are aware or unaware that our behaviors are under the influence of the mold?*

**A:** If we become aware of the deceit and interference of the "I" or the "mold," this very awareness changes the quality of our relationships. Possibly to date you have been unaware of the mold's interference in your communications. Consequently, all your relations have had a narrow quality of ignorance. Prejudice is the result of ignorance and unconsciousness. However, now you have become aware that your relations are not immune to the "mold's" interferences. This awareness alone gives you an inner humility. Viewpoints and narratives rooted in humility feel very different from prejudiced views and narratives. Maybe until now you have thought that your opinions, evaluations, logic, values, beliefs, and all your attachments and mental content are the most accurate and righteous. But now you have become aware that your conclusions and perceptions have been based on criteria and standards that are untrustworthy, flawed, and not even yours to begin with. Considering this, will you show grudge and prejudice in your discussions with others?

**Q:** *I say either there is a mold or there isn't. If there is a mold in our minds, it enters and interferes with all of our relations.*

**A:** No, it does not always happen. It only happens when we have *identified* ourselves (due to lack of awareness) with the subject in review. In examining a rock or a plant, you have the mold identity. In examining a system of morals, you also have the mold. But is your mind's *quality* the same when examining these two subjects? In examining a rock, the mold exists, but it does not interject itself into your view and observation of the rock. There is no personal interest originating from the "I" and projecting outward toward the rock. You do not think, "Since this is a well-bred, honest, and respectful rock, and there is a kind of relationship and dependency between me and this rock, then I am a proponent of its authenticity." You are much more likely to look at the subject without a conditioned framework. You can relate to the rock with a whole and open mind, (I use the expression "whole mind" as the opposite to a "fragmented mind,") and so you simply examine the rock, without any need to defend its honor and glory.

However, the same cannot be said about your views toward a philosophical subject or system of morals—because we usually assume a relationship with philosophical and moral systems, and this assumed relationship obscures our views and makes us biased toward the subject. As soon as we form a relationship with the subject, a true examination is null and the problem of taking sides and dogmatically defending the correctness of our views begins to dominate the relationship.

Now, when you are examining a system of morality, if you are aware that through creating a personal connection to the topic you are interjecting your own mental interpretations, this simple awareness cuts off that sense of personal relationship, and you can look at that system as though you look at a rock or a plant.

**Q:** *A rock or a plant is different from a social system or system of morals. Can a human being examine, for instance, the communist system, with the same view as he would examine a rock?*

**A:** What's important is not the subject in review but rather our minds' qualities. It is important to be aware of our mental quality while looking at a subject. If we look at the communist system or any other social system without the "I's" interference, we can examine it as we would a rock. Every system of morals has its own reality, along with some embellishments our minds have created. If we remove these embellishments, what remains is pure reality. And this pure reality can be examined in the same way that we examine a rock.

**Q:** *So we must not bring up philosophical subjects? Don't you think that if we look at problems with a philosophical perspective, we might find a better solution for them?*

**A:** A philosophical discussion is different from having a philosophical view or insight. We do not normally live from the philosophical view. We do big philosophical discussions, and our talks and theories are high level, but the content of our own lives is small. We are involved in very small problems that are personal and bounded. For example, we may be discussing philosophy and the emptiness of life, but as soon as we hear that a friend has not invited us to his party, this matter keeps our minds preoccupied with grudges for days and even months. Our real lives are filled with multitudes of such petty problems, even if in theory we prefer to talk about subjects of greater import such as philosophy or metaphysics. I would prefer that instead of philo-sophical discussions, we would have some philosophical *insight* in relation to our lives. If we had greater philosophical insight, perhaps we would not be caught up with the "self" and its petty concerns, and we would not think this so called "preciousness" is the center of the universe and everything must revolve around it. I would prefer that we might realize the reality of our lifetimes in comparison to the eternity of all existence, rather than to what has been and what will be. These short, precious lifetimes are but a blink of an eye. If we could find such a view we would let go of this fabrication of an "I" and not cling to it day and night.

# CHAPTER EIGHT

# KNOW THE WORLD FROM KNOWING THE SELF

C onsidering the subjects of the previous chapter, I hope that our discussions can now stay free of grudge, prejudice, and prejudgment. Prejudgment distorts our view of reality like a blurry shadow. It's possible for us to look at all subjects freshly, as they are in this moment, as if seeing them for the first time. When all prior understanding is put aside, everything appears fresh and whole. If we look at subjects from the point of view of prior understanding, our investigation will be biased, and the need for justifying our prior conclusions will arise, in which case nothing will become any clearer. Each one of us will be throwing our previous understandings at each other without any beneficial results.

\*\*\*

**Q:** *In my opinion, throughout all our discussions you have generally investigated subjects from a singular point of view.*

# THE POWER OF NO THOUGHT

*You look at the problems of human beings only from a psychological perspective, without considering other aspects. There is no doubt that competition causes many problems, as you have pointed out, but have you ever thought about the history behind where competition began and what the initial cause was?*

**A:** In my opinion, discovering the initial cause of competition would not help us much. It is important to see why competition exists now and how we can get rid of it. If my house is on fire, my immediate problem is to extinguish the fire, not to find out who set the house on fire and for what reason. All our preoccupations, ploys, and self-deceptions are gathered around us so that we will not see the burning house. We do not sense the gravity of our lives passing by. If we could comprehend the seriousness of this matter, we would relinquish our amusement in other preoccupations and would pay attention to the problem with everything we've got.

Searching for historical causes is only an avoidance of the existing problem and our fear of what we might discover. In order to postpone seeing the existing problem, thought keeps itself busy with extraneous subjects like history and various other fixations so as to avoid the actual problem. When the mind goes after historical reasons, it is keeping itself busy with theories and opinions related to the problem while continuously skirting the heart of the matter. These are two very different approaches. The reality of the problem is one thing and theories related to that are something else. *Actuality* describes the present, while *theory* drags the mind into time. And every movement that the mind makes in time is exactly the continuation of the problem. (Again,

I reiterate that our discussion is about psychological matters, not physical and material.)

**Q:** *Is it possible that the same reasons that initially created the problem presently exist and are the causes of its continuation?*

**A:** Even if that were not the case, we would still want to look at those reasons as the cause of the current problem. I want to emphasize that I am not approaching these subjects from a *philosophical* viewpoint; because in philosophy, due to the principle of movement, no one cause can always be considered the reason. Every cause functions only for a very short period of time before giving way to another cause. Every effect becomes a cause for the next effect. Therefore, finding a cause requires halting the movement for a moment.

For example, let's assume that the area in which we live is a marshland. The swamp becomes the cause for malaria-carrying mosquitos. (The mosquitos are the effect of the swamp.) Then a mosquito bites you and the virus enters your body. (The mosquito is the cause and the virus is the effect.) Next you get a fever. (The virus is the cause and the fever is the effect.) To treat your fever, we examine the virus, not the swamp. But, if we want to examine the swamp itself, we should examine the cause for the swamp's creation rather than examining the effects of the swamp, or our task will continue on forever.

**Q:** *Don't you think our existing "virus" is the monopolization and unjust distribution of the wealth? Couldn't this problem be the foundation and the initial cause of all problems? In my opinion, if we could get rid of monopolization and injustice in* *the distribution of society's wealth, all the problems that have ensued from this foundational problem would be removed.*

**A:** Let's see how much of this subject is correct and how much is incorrect. There is no doubt that there is monopolization and injustice in distribution of wealth, exploitation of humans by humans, and many such problems of this nature. If we consider any criterion and logic in this regard, we see that the current situation and the relationship between production and distribution are incongruent and unreasonable. Any discrepancy and disharmony in one aspect of our relationship with all of life affects every other aspect while disrupting the harmony of the whole.

For instance, we may say that God has created all humans equal. Well, this is not just a gratuitous statement. Being equal means that we should all benefit equally from society's privileges. However, on a practical level it is not like that. For some, "equal before the law" is only a complimentary statement, not the reality, because others reap the actual benefits. And this matter obstructs the order of all our social relations.

Hence, there is no doubt that there is injustice and it should be eradicated, but to think that solving this problem will resolve all the problems of humanity is not plausible, as there are even greater foundational problems. And besides, our experience shows contradictory results. In some societies economic monopolization and material exploitation have been eradicated, but don't they still have problems? Have individuals in those societies realized their humanity in the truest sense?

I hope that after these discussions we will have established a clear and comprehensive understanding of a healthy human being and a healthy society, and that we do not see man's problems as bound to only a few small and superficial causes. A healthy society is not solely about eating equally, dressing equally, attending school equally, benefiting from medicine and treatment equally, enjoying entertainment equally, etc. A healthy society provides opportunities to all people so that they can flourish in their individuality, including educational and cultural systems that do not prevent an individual's independence and inner freedoms (of much greater importance than outer freedoms).

Such a society does not make its people obedient slaves to propaganda, does not render individuals powerless and unconscious, and does not hinder the nourishment of love in the true sense (not love for your country and hate for another, love for your own type and hate for the other, etc.). Do you know of such a society? Let's optimistically assume that there is equal opportunity and social benefits in some countries and due to the existence of a government and system of justice, the people of those countries do not exploit each other. But if there were such societies, this would only be true inside the borders of those countries, and still they can easily exploit people outside their borders. Whereas human beings who in truth know that they are not separate from others do not exploit others, be they Russian, American, or Arab.

The reason that man has not been able to practically bring an idealistic heaven to life is that this imaginary heaven comes from the "I," and there is never a pure intention in the substance of the "I." *The self is an entirely ignorant phenomenon. And an ignorant phenomenon cannot be the source of benevolence.* It is like the devil wanting to create heaven on earth. All movements and aspirations issued by the "I" are wicked and foul. The "I" basically does not know benevolence. As long as we are living with the "I," we cannot be sincere in our claim of wanting to create heaven on earth.

*My point is, let's purify our spiritual beings before anything else. So long as we have not purified ourselves of the ignorance of our true nature, there is no hope that goodness and benevolence flow from our actions.*

**Q:** *Why should one bother with good intentions? If you want to build a bridge, good intentions are of no significance. Scientific knowledge and correct observations are all we need.*

**A:** Let's assume that for building a bridge, there is no need for good intentions. Building a society, on the other hand, is not comparable to building a bridge. These two do not have similar qualities. For building a society, love is necessary. *Any action that does not come from love is incongruent and inharmonious.* It may fix one corner but then at the same time damage others. Any function that does not have its roots in love is rooted in the "I," and all destructive characteristics of the "I" will accompany it.

**Q:** *Then what should we do? Is it right that in spite of all the injustice around us, we merely sit and talk quietly?*

**A:** I do not say that we should not take action. I only say that we should know the "actor" so that the action will come from consciousness and kindness. An action that comes from the "I" is not only blind; it also lacks kindness. The phenomenon of thought identity, due to its substance and its system of values, does not basically know true kindness. Thought identity is based on viciousness.

154

KNOW THE WORLD FROM KNOWING THE SELF

All we need to do is consider a few characteristics of the "I" and observe how these negative characteristics enter every aspect of our lives, our relationships, and our activities, and interject an unnatural and meaningless quality. For example, just see what conflict does to us! We know that one of the results of conflict is that it makes our lives empty of direction and higher goals and causes us to not want anything seriously and wholeheartedly. You can carefully look at the behaviors of people around you and see how this characteristic (conflict) gives an incongruent and self-absorbed quality to their behaviors.

A few nights ago I was a guest of a young fellow who used to be a member of a communist party. We were discussing how disgusting it was for humans to exploit other humans. Meanwhile, he was constantly ordering about his elderly servant lady, and the poor lady, due to her old age, could not walk briskly but she was forced to obey in order to earn a loaf of bread.

I know another person who is a millionaire and a proponent of wealth distribution, but not for one moment would he halt his plans to become a billionaire.

You might have observed such scenes in a park where young fellows force other kids off the swings so that they can sit together and start a discussion about freedom. These are just some examples of the good intentions of the human "I." And this type of meaningless and self-absorbed behavior is not specific to any one group of people.

We all have the same conditioning but with different form and content. The examples that I've mentioned here represent only a few of thought identity's characteristics. There are scores of other characteristics within the destructive system of thought identity, and each one impairs an aspect of our natural being. So, with this "I" that is full of problems, how can we fundamentally solve any other problem? As long as we have not solved the problem of the self, we cannot essentially solve anything else! This is my point.

**Q:** *Let's assume that monopolization and exploitation are not foundational problems. In your opinion, isn't the poverty that comes from the unjust distribution of wealth important enough to seriously do something about its eradication?*

**A:** Of course, it is necessary. Aside from psychological aspects, poverty resulting from monopolization and exploitation is not an insignificant problem. It contributes to psychological pain as well as the pain of being hungry. Resolving mental pain is every individual's responsibility, and we should all work on our individual psychological pain.. However, hunger is a social problem and to eradicate it, a society must take constructive action, not destructive.

**Q:** *You are saying that to eradicate hunger, a social movement should take place. My point is that you also say that any talk or movement toward slowing down or derailing such a problem is harmful.*

**A:** Which one of the comments that I mentioned, interferes with such a movement? Isn't it necessary for any useful social movement for people to initially be conscious human beings? Shouldn't individuals in a society reach a level of consciousness that enables them to recognize certain rights for themselves as human beings? Shouldn't they know what right means, what freedom means, what exploitation means? *We must first become conscious, and then act from consciousness.* By doing so, our actions will be positive and constructive, not revengeful and destructive. Optimally, this action is issued from a conscious and righteous human being, not from the "I."

What I'm saying is that the mental mold that the "I" is made of hinders the wholeness of true consciousness. If you break this mold and look at life without it, everything finds a quality and manifestation beyond compare to your current reality. The mold causes us to see only one step ahead, meaning, that it limits our view, and as we are fascinated and absorbed with it, we cannot see anything outside of the mold's framework and contents. The mold gives our minds a habitual quality, meaning that the mind becomes accustomed to looking at life's affairs and circumstances only from certain angles permitted by the mold. If our molds were removed, we could see many things that presently cannot be seen!

There are problems in all societies, and each society's specific social mold prevents its people from seeing the depths of its problems and aggravations as they really are. We can read in history books that throughout time human beings have been bought and sold. How surprising this is for us. It is hard to believe that human beings were once thought of as commodities that could be bought and sold. But for people living in those times, this was a completely normal matter. This is because the people of those times had been kept in a specific mold that didn't allow them to see it as anything abnormal. Whatever mold was imposed upon them would be seen as a normal affair, and they would believe that this was how things were supposed to be.

And it's true for us at the present time. You and I also see many circumstances that seem completely normal to us, and this is due to being accustomed to our specific upbringing and environment, to our specific mold. Our circumstances may seem unbelievable to people a hundred years from now, and they will ask themselves how it was possible that in some parts of earth people suffered from starvation while in another part of the same planet the excess crops were burned?! But for us now, this problem appears to be a normal state of affairs.

The reason that people of every age do not feel the depths of the issues of their time is that they are absorbed in the mold of their generation, and the mold justifies everything for them. But the people of another age that do not have the same mold and justifications will have a different quality of seeing.

If we were to see our current problems from outside the mold of our times, they would seem unbearable for even a second. Then of course we would try to resolve them in a conscious, productive, and logical way. However, presently we are not able to see their depths. We just make some noise and small actions that satisfy our seeming need for hatred and violence in the name of peace and intellectual responsibility.

When any action arises from the "I," what is paramount in that moment is the "self," not the action. For the one who is identified by thought, the dearest and the most important thing is the self. Such a being is a "self-centered" slave, and everything revolves around the self, whether overtly or covertly. And we know some of the characteristics of this self are based on anger and disgust. Anger and disgust are hidden behind every action, behavior, and goal that comes from the self, although disguised and justified by beautiful wrappings.

For example, we often say, "Let us rise against exploiters and reclaim the rights of those who are exploited." We claim that we want to improve the situation of those who are exploited, but secretly our goal is more targeted at destroying the exploiters. We never think about improving the lives of both, and this is because the "structure" of our beings has a destructive quality. We always want to ruin somebody's house.

Perhaps you have noticed how excitedly we rise in support or opposition to an individual or a group. As soon as we win a situation in support of an individual or a group, we start a fight against some other individuals or groups.

**Q:** *I have a couple of questions that are a bit off topic. My first question is from what age do active thoughts become dominant over our existence?*

**A:** Do you want to examine your questions one by one or all together?

**Q:** *Perhaps one by one is better.*

**A:** Before I answer, I'd like to ask what the purpose of the question is. What result would you want to obtain from your question? It's possible for a question to be basically futile, and then we are forced to discuss a futile subject, which does not help us. I'm not saying that your question is futile, but first let's see how it might help us if we clarify the subject of your question. We do not want to add to our coffers of psychological information and knowledge; and our goal is not to prove any theory. We want insight into the true nature of our beings and the workings of our minds. And this job is not going to get fixed by psychological assumptions and theories, even if the theories are correct.

So to begin with, let's clarify that active thoughts influence the mind from the age of one or ten. By knowing this, what do you want to conclude?

**Q:** *Suppose I have an eight-year-old son, and I want to know whether interpretive thinking is influencing him. If yes, what could I do to help him stay immune to it and the pain and suffering of thought identity?*

**A:** First you should clarify whether thought identity is dominant over *your* own being and relationships or not.

**Q:** *Certainly it is.*

**A:** Considering your answer, how can you help your child to stay immune from the effects of this phenomenon? Our relationships with all life, including our children, are influenced by thought identity. This is our basic way of being and we don't know anything other than this. Therefore, our means of communication with others cannot be anything but an ultimately unnatural and negative force.

I am surprised by those who write books with titles such as "How to educate your child." All of these books should be about educating us as a human race. The problem is *us,* not the child. If we could get rid of the mold of thought identity for ourselves, our lives, our behaviors, and our relationships would enjoy a useful, rational, and harmonious quality. And then there would be no need to ask others how we should educate our children. *A healthy spiritual being will automatically result in a healthy spiritual upbringing.* But as long as the mold identity has its grip on us, reading thousands of educational books and guides will have no effect. What we learn as theories from these books simply become "ideal" patterns for us, yet still in our relationships with others we relate from the standpoint of who and what we think we are.

**Q:** *But after becoming aware that the "I" is a destructive force, can't we keep a child immune from its effects?*

**A:** It depends on the quality of our awareness. If our awareness has increased to the extent that we have experienced the aggravation and unnaturalness of the "I" with our whole being, we must free ourselves from it first and then we can relate to the world as a free being filled with love. If our awareness has not reached the extent that we are ready to let go of this so called gift, this means that we have yet to find it aggravating enough, and we still see its existence as a necessary means for the self.

**Q:** *Are you saying that after we learn about the harmful effects of competition, we cannot educate our children to renounce competition and a competitive life?*

**A:** Not completely. We may, after understanding competition's disadvantages, discourage the child from competition. However, in the way we conduct our lives, we might unknowingly move the child towards a competitive life. I may consciously acknowledge that I do not want my child to get familiar with competition; however, if the root of my subconscious being is still connected to competition, then this influences the child even more than by my conscious decisions.

**Q:** *So are you saying that as long as we have the mold of thought identity, we cannot help but project that mold onto our children?*

**A:** The mold is always a part of the mind, though it may interfere with some relationships more than others.

In the previous chapter I said that the mold enters into a relationship when the mind creates an attachment between the mold and the subject, meaning that the mold identifies with the subject. For example, you may be watching a wrestling match on TV between a Russian and an American. Another day you see a Persian wrestling a Russian. In watching both matches your mold is operating, but is the quality of your mind and your feeling while watching both matches the same? Obviously not. In watching the wrestling match between the Russian and the American, your mind might be impartial, which means the mold has not infected your view. But in watching the wrestling between the Russian and the Persian (assuming that you are Persian), your mind is *biased* due to your attachment to the Persian nationality.

If you do not create an attachment between yourself and other things, you see them with a clear and unbiased view, meaning without interference of the mold. However, in relation to your child, you certainly have a relationship of attachment, and therefore your approach to his education cannot stay immune from the interference of the mold.

**Q:** *It feels as though you are completely negating education.*

**A:** No, you are misunderstanding. First, I hope you do not mistake "education" for "upbringing." I should provide all means possible for my child's education. I should teach him two plus two equals four, how electricity is created, how to drive a car, etc.

If I did not know two plus two equals four, or if I did not know the laws of physics, would you see me as a suitable teacher? Obviously not. You would tell me that first I need to learn math and physics before I can teach your child.

But shouldn't this be obvious in regards to upbringing as well? If I want to raise my child properly, wouldn't I first need to train myself properly? As long as I live with thought identity, I will basically not have any personal experience to pass on to my child.

So I'm not negating the need for a proper upbringing. I'm only saying that I should initially find the truth for myself before I can benefit anyone else.

**Q:** *Suppose I smoke or I lie habitually. Shouldn't my child understand that smoking or lying is bad?*

**A:** First, some of these examples are in the domain of science. Second, you are saying to the child, by words and apparently by good intention, that smoking or lying is bad, but your whole unconscious relationship with these tendencies implicitly encourages the child in the direction of smoking or lying.

I would like to clarify this point further. You are saying that you want to raise your child properly, even better than you were yourself. You want him to not have undesirable characteristics that you yourself may have. Certainly, your father had the same goal and intention in relation to your own upbringing. And your grandfather had the same intention for your father. You can follow the same trend back to your ancestors. This means that our ancestors have all tried to bring up their children better than they themselves were brought up. So, if these "better upbringings" were effective in practice, the world would be filled with saints. Unfortunately, however, we can see that the world is the same hell as it was a thousand years ago, just a different kind of hell that reflects our current stage of evolution.

I hope that those who consider morality in a relative sense, meaning on a scale of better or worse, will be cognizant of this. If relativity exists in spiritual matters, that relativity will be moving in a direction.

**Q:** *Maybe in our case this relativity has moved towards getting worse.*

**A:** The truth is that the situation has not gotten better or worse. When we look at circumstances through the lens of "single occurrence," it may seem that a particular event or type of life is better or worse than another. But if we were to look with a broader and more holistic view, we would see that our lives have a stagnated, swamp-like quality. Some people have always been seeking a "better" mirage, but the human condition has remained the same, out of touch with his true nature, though we have been acting and pretending to carry higher human values.

Let me explain further. We sometimes hear moral and religious slogans that we believe in, but we do not adopt them in our own actions. Thus there's really no practical difference between knowing and not knowing, believing and not believing. For example, you may have heard some sage say, "Bring up your children in a way that's appropriate for their times." How do we practically use this advice? Don't we ask ourselves what did that sage really mean by that statement?

If you had no familiarity with that statement, would hearing it change the way you're currently relating with your children? Do you think you should bring them up in accordance with their times? If so, is it possible for you to say how you would practically implement this idea? How can you bring them up for their times when you are trying to transfer your own mental mold into their minds?

**Q:** *On a slightly different note, has modern life not taken away from our basic spiritual understanding of ourselves and created more disagreements among humans?*

**A:** First of all, no. Seven hundred years ago, the armies of Timor Lang were fighting with bows and arrows, and today people fight with atomic bombs. The essence of the fighting has not changed. Humans with unnatural and hateful qualities always use the latest weapons against one another.

Secondly, suppose modern inventions and the industrial revolution have worsened our understanding of who we are as spiritual beings. By that assumption, we should ask the question, why have we allowed ourselves to be affected by what we have built and let it determine our fate, our spirit, and our relationships? The thought-identified human gets easily influenced, as our lives are not grounded in anything real. If it had not been machinery, we would have created something else that would have ruled us to the same degree.

# CHAPTER NINE

# REMOVE SELF-DECEPTION; IT IS IN THE WAY

T hrough my explanation in the previous chapters, it should be evident by now how thought identity inter-jects itself and becomes the ruler of our lives. Still, I would like to describe this phenomenon one more time in the hopes that it will become undeniably clear.

We know that our means of relating with life is through thought. We also know that the quality at which this tool current-ly functions is not flawless and trouble-free. One's thought is mixed with delusion and is alterable, uncertain, and often nega-tive. Therefore our problem, more than anything, is the means of thought itself. As long as this altered means is not corrected, all aspects of our lives and our relations with God, with each other, with morality, and with society will have a dark quality.

If you and I are talking on the phone, and the quality of our voices is degraded due to transmission issues in the connection, the first thing we will do is try to fix the connection.

We should do the same thing for our minds. The mind is our means of communications with the external world. Hence, we should first assure ourselves that this instrument is working correctly.

Right now I am speaking about certain subjects and you are hearing me. We are relating through the use of our minds. Words and expressions from my mind enter your minds exactly like transmitter and receiver devices. So shouldn't we, before we try to communicate, make sure that the devices are working properly?

Therefore, our task is to attune the instrument. As long as this instrument is not in proper working condition, any assessment, any examination, and any judgment made by us will be uncertain. Considering this fact, I hope from now on all your questions will be about how to correct the instrument. Some individuals ask, for example, "Is this system of thought better than the others?" "Is the individual more important than the society?" "Is this society healthier than the other one?" and so on. Before attempting to respond, we should bring up the question of whether the instrument we are examining with, the tool that should clarify and resolve those problems, is working properly. This is our task.

\*\*\*

**Q:** *If the means of communication is working correctly for some people, can they not clarify social problems for others?*

**A:** Assume that your mind, meaning your examination tool, is functioning properly, and therefore all personal and social problems are clear in your mind. But my mind is not like that. Now, please tell me exactly how can you help me?

**Q:** *If I can see social problems clearly, then I can help you and others to see more.*

**A:** Please pay attention to your supposition of the problem. We're assuming that your mind is clear and my mind is dark, and you want to help me see life's problems clearly. But the clarity of your mind is definite only for you, not for me. How can I discern, with my clouded mind, that your mind is clear and what you say is the truth? Do you understand my question?

**Q:** *Yes. You are saying that with a clouded mind you cannot discern the quality of the other person's mind, even if that person's mind is really clear. But I think this subject is exaggerated. To what extent could the mind be clouded that it cannot discern clear and obvious truths?*

**A:** That which is obvious truth to you may not have occurred to another. Where are all disagreements and conflicts among human beings coming from? Everybody perceives his/her own delusions as obvious truths and is biased towards them.

Let's optimistically assume that the clarity of your mind has become certain to me too. In this case, how should you help me see the truth clearly in life? Your help is only real when it can remove factors of darkness from my mind so that I can see the truths for myself with a clear mind. Meaning, your help should eventually be in the direction of clearing my mind; otherwise, your help wouldn't be effective.

Our help to each other is not usually help. You want to describe the truths that you have seen. Therefore, assuming that your descriptions are the exact truth, they might still be useless for me. It could be the case that you have directly seen the truth, but I have only heard the *description* of the truth. What you have seen as the truth and what I have heard about the truth are theories related to the truth. And theories related to things are different from the reality of the thing, even when the theories are according to the truths. That's what we mean when we say we are "second hand" human beings. We do not have lucid minds, but we relate to life and its problems through others' theories and opinions.

I hope with these explanations the problem has become clearer for us, and we know in which direction we should move. Our most important problem is our own self-delusion. As long as we do not resolve the problem of the self, our lives and our behaviors will have a blind quality.

Now let's bring up opinions or questions in this context and avoid unrelated subjects that would not help resolve the problem of the self.

***

**Q:** *Can we draw the conclusion that your emphasis is on the personal, individual effort and therefore you do not consider social sciences credible?*

**A:** Do not rely on my opinion. See for yourself whether it is credible or not. What we have been discussing is a universal matter that relates to sociology as well. Firstly, have sociologists examined and described the laws that govern societies with correct means? Secondly, assuming that the sociologists' investigations have had the correct approach and their conclusions are truthful, how do we benefit from those conclusions when our minds are clouded? *Every movement of a psychologist, sociologist, philosopher, or anybody else should be in the direction of clearing their own ignorance; otherwise all movement in any direction would just be a continuation of that.*

So, if you agree with me that our most important job is self-realization, then let us limit our questions and discussions to this subject only.

**Q:** *Other than the ways that you have already mentioned, is there any simpler way to self-realization?*

**A:** There is nothing in the way of self-realization. Our problem is to want it or not to want it. If we really want to know ourselves, we find the way. The problem is that we are *afraid* of knowing ourselves and would prefer to stay in darkness. Considering this, how would it make a difference whether there is one way to self-realization or a hundred ways; whether the ways are simple or difficult? You are standing outside of a city, and for some reason you are afraid of entering the city, so you stand outside the city and ask others the best and easiest way into the city. Isn't it like this?

Our minds have become accustomed from early childhood to constantly be thinking about "having," "being" and "becoming." The one thing we know for sure is that we need to be something or to become something. Thus we have a fear of "being nothing." We do not want to lose our identity, which we have gotten accustomed to over thirty or forty years, and living without that identity is utterly unthinkable. For us, not having an identity is like psychological death, and we fear this as much as physical death. Outwardly, we say that we are ready to lose thought iden-

171

tity, but inwardly we are attached to it. We push it away with one hand and pull it back with the other! In this regard, Rumi states:

هم به هوای جلوه ای پاره کنم حجاب را
هم به نگاه نارسا پرده کشم به روی تو

*In desire to see your face I rip the veil,*
*Yet hide away my eyes from your face.*

Desire is on the one hand but fear is on the other! We say we aspire to self-realization, but what we really want is a more magnificent "I." When we hear about the possibility of self-realization, we try to conjure up an image of the ideal man without identity, and then we desire to trade in our present mold identity for the new image. Doing this hasn't changed the essence of the matter. A new mold in place of an older mold is still a mold, described with different terms and expressions.

**Q:** *Then how can we reach the state of no-identity, despite the fear of letting go of the "I," and despite the fact that we always keep some image of it in a corner of our minds?*

**A:** The essence of your statement is this: "Intellectually I have realized that entering the city does not have any danger, but my habit and my fear blocks me from entering the city." Now, you would like to find a way to automatically enter the city. In other words, to find a way to trap and destroy thought identity.

**Q:** *That's exactly what I meant.*

**A:** The only trap is *awareness about thought activities and movements of the mind*, without rejecting it or accepting it. Meaning, without labeling one thought as good and another as bad. If we pay attention to our mental interactions during wake-fulness, the "I" does not remain in the mind. Again, I should remind you that the "I" is nothing separate from the active pursuit of thought and roaming around in time. Therefore if thought is continuously in the present, it becomes empty of an "I."

**Q:** *To distinguish when thought is in the state of attention and awareness and when it is free-wheeling and fantasizing is difficult.*

**A:** To distinguish or not is not important. Presently some thoughts are happening in your mind. Be aware of those thoughts, whatever they are, fantasizing, vain thoughts, real thoughts or anything else. Be alert and conscious of your own thought movements. *That's it.*

**Q:** *The problem is that I can attend to thoughts for a few seconds or a few minutes and then notice that I have involuntarily lost attention. In the meantime, the mind has been busy fantasizing for hours, without awareness.*

**A:** Pay attention to the lack of attention as well. Recognize that you aren't paying attention, and in every way possible, bring awareness to the movements of the mind.

**Q:** *Who is it that pays attention? It seems to me that the agent of attention is thought itself. One thought just follows another thought.*

**A:** We cannot say that these are actually two thoughts, one following the other. *The state of awareness and pure attention is not thought. Rather, it is an "insight" with a quality of intelligence.* Mental contents that arise from memory are what we call thoughts; but in the state of *insight awareness* no thought is arising from the memory or referring to memory. This situation is

like a trap that suffocates the "I." Rumi describes these two processes and mental interactions as "partial intellect" and "whole
intellect."

عقل جزیی عشق را منکر بود
گرچه بنماید که صاحب سر بود
زیرك و داناست اما نیست، نیست
تا فرشته لا نشد اهریمنی است
او به قول و فعل یار ما بود
چون به حکم حال آیی لا بود

*The partial intellect denies love,*
*Though it pretends to own the self.*

*It thinks it is clever and wise but it is not,*
*So far from being an angel, it is the devil.*

*It stays with us by chatting and interaction,*
*When it comes to the present, it does not exist.*

The "partial intellect" refers to the compartmentalization and
fragmentation that goes on within the mind. Before the mind becomes a nest for delusional thoughts of an "I," it functions as a
full-length mirror and a whole unit. After partitioning, every part
of the mind serves one of the "Is" by being a proxy for it. Therefore the mind keeps itself busy with pieces of the whole, thus its
activities always have a fragmented quality. To say that "The
partial intellect denies love" conveys that each part of the fragmented intellect or thought is rooted in and has arisen from the
"I." Further, every thought attached to the "I" is lacking love.

174

The partial thought is clever, practiced, and tricky; but since it is "something" rather than "nothing," since it does not have a "non-existent" quality, it has a foul or negative quality.

**Q:** *Then how does one discern between the partial intellect and the whole intellect? The apparent meaning of these two in terms is clear, but it seems to me very hard to intuit what is partial intellect and what is whole intellect.*

**A:** If we use the terms partial thought and whole thought instead of partial intellect and whole intellect, the problem may become clearer.

You ask, when does thought have a partial quality and when a whole quality? All thoughts are partial. Every movement of the mind and every event that is based on a subject/object relationship is partial, whereas a mind with a quality of wholeness does not experience any separation between itself and the object of its perceiving.

For instance, you may be thinking about a tree. The tree is both an object in your mind and the subject of your thinking. The next moment, you may be thinking about something else, such as how you are an educated or an ignorant person, how you have self-pity or pride, and whatever attributes you feel you have or don't have. Even when your thought creates an "I" that does not have a certain attribute, it still, in fact, has an "affirmative" quality, but in the form of "lack/want." (You must not mistake the mind's negative quality with the quality of "nothingness".)

All these attributes—knowledge, ignorance, self-pity, and so on—are the objects of your thoughts. Now if your mind absolutely does not perceive any object, not a real object like a tree or a mental object such as knowledge, then what quality does it have? It has the quality of "nothingness" or space. And this quality is the absence of "I," meaning that the mind is empty of the "I." Because the "I" is comprised of those objects that thought has been thinking about; and when no thought object is present, the mind will be free from barriers and will realize a quality of boundless, infinite and wholeness. And that's the end of it.

**Q:** *In order to free the mind from thinking about partial things and personal, partial objects, Gnostics say to always remember God, because God is the whole without any personal quality.*

**A:** I do not exactly know what Gnostics say in this regard. Just don't be fooled by thought. Do not create a God from your partial thoughts, and do not consider your delusional thoughts to know God. No thought can be in relation to the infinite and the absolute. *The partial thought is a veil between you and the infinite; therefore the veil must first be removed, and then your being dissolves into the infinite and becomes one with it.*

I think the content of this message from Rumi conveys this experience:

زین وصیت کرد ما را مصطفی
بحث کم جویید در ذات خدا
آنکه در ذاتش تفکر کرد نیست
در حقیقت آن نظر در ذات نیست
هست آن پندار او، زیرا به راه
صد هزاران پرده آمد تا اله
هر یکی در پرده ای موصول جست
وهم او آنست کآن خود عین اوست

*Hence the prophet instructed us,*
*Do not seek discussion about the essence of God.*

*In regards to that one whose essence is an object of thought,*
*In reality the thinker's speculation is not concerning the es-*
*sence.*

*This is only his delusion, because on the way to God,*
*There are a hundred thousand veils.*

*Everyone is attached to some veil,*
*And judges that as his own identity.*

Consider this point carefully. As I have mentioned previously, in order to avoid self-deception, be alert that your mind
should not have a seeking quality! Do not look for anything, because whatever you are looking for is a creation of your own
delusion. It's like you have thrown delusion before yourself, and
now you are chasing it, all the while imagining that you are looking for something new. You have just put a new word and a new
name on an old delusion, and now you are looking for the same
old delusion, albeit with new words. As long as the means of
your seeking is the mold, you will not find anything new—
because the mold is old and whatever is sought and found by this
old means has the old quality of the mold.

One of the most important plots of thought identity is to
cause us to use an old, dead instrument through which to view
our dynamic and continually renewing existence. Rumi has

many times pointed out this fundamental and destructive characteristic of thought identity.

ور بگیری نکته ای بکر و لطیف

بعد درکت گشت بی ذوق و کثیف

*If you capture a subtle and authentic idea in your thought,*
*The depth of your perception will end up contaminated and*
*soulless.*

As a new thing enters the domain of the self, when perceived
with an old and static tool, the self makes an old thing from the
new, devoid of delight and freshness. The self then becomes
soulless, exactly like sorrow. Again Rumi says:

چیز دیگر تازه و نو گفته گیر

باز فردا ز آن شوی سیر و نفیر

*Today you look to find some other thing new and fresh,*
*Only tomorrow to be filled with it and despise it.*

Our feelings of boredom, of being disheartened, dejected,
and so on, are due to our old and uninspired existence. We are
always after something new—new experiences, thrills, and different understandings—but soon after attaining these, we are
again bored with what we have.

Here, Rumi provides a permanent solution to our predicament:

178

# REMOVE SELF-DECPTION; IT IS IN THE WAY

دفع علت کن، چو علت خو شود
هر حدیث کهنه پیشت نو شود

*Reject the cause that is nested in you,*
*And old stories before you will be new.*

"Reject the cause" means to reject the "I." The "I" is the cause of illness.

**Q:** *Is it possible to seek this realization without the mold?*

**A:** In seeking, you are looking for something, for some kind of object you feel is hidden from your view. What impression do you have of this thing, and by what means would you hope to obtain that thing? Are there any means besides the mold? Let's assume that you want to look for "love" or "truth." The very seeking of love indicates that you believe it to be somewhere outside of you. You are not feeling the state or content of love. So, in seeking for love, you are after the *delusion* of love. You have drawn a picture of love with your mold, and now you are after the drawing that the mold has created for you.

**Q:** *If it were like this, then the only thing we would find is something fixed and petrified, much like the mold, meaning that we would not get to anything new.*

**A:** No, not exactly. From one perspective the mold does not get petrified; it gradually inflates. However this inflation has a quality of multiplication. This means that the mold multiplies itself, and we see these multiplications as something new. However, whatever seems new to us is in fact not new, meaning completely fresh and intact. Whatever it is, it is still a product of the previous mold, and hence has the color and substance of the previous mold.

Here is a simple example that will help to clarify this for you:

When a shallow and tasteless poet wants to write a new poem, he puts all his best effort, capacity, and talent to create an excellent poem. Once he has created his poem, though it is a new poem, it may still have the same tasteless quality as his previous poems. This is because his new poem has been written within the same framework as his old mold and brought forth from the same ingredients as his previous tasteless poems.

The mind must become empty of the "I." And once you recognize that *a striving mind only strengthens the "I,"* then the mind stops striving to "become." When the mind stops trying to become, it has become empty of the "I." *The very activity and striving of thought has been the reason for the "I's" existence all along.* If there is no seeking and striving, the "I" no longer exists. Rumi expresses this in this verse:

چون نپرسی زودتر کشفت شود
مرغ صبر از جمله پران تر بود

*Your discoveries will be sooner when query is naught,*
*The bird of patience flies to an all higher height.*

Without any intention of "becoming," we need only be aware of our mental activity. The mind must rest in its essential quality of awareness, not striving to become or to desire for anything whatsoever. An image of becoming requires thinking in

180

time, and through striving, the intention of becoming remains hidden. Every movement of the mind in time is nothing but the continuation of the "I."

**Q:** *What factors and conditions would help us to realize this truth?*

**A:** Do you mean internal or external factors?

**Q:** *Any kind of condition or factor, internal or external. For example, is it better to seek for the truth in seclusion and solitude, or in a crowd and among social relationships? What effect might certain conditions have in the search for self-realization, such as the level of intelligence, literacy, age, and so on?*

**A:** Age has some effect due to the long habit of living with thought identity. The older we get, the harder the task becomes.

In regards to seclusion and living in solitude, some imagine that if we leave society and go to the mountaintops or the deserts, we might realize ourselves more quickly. This is a common path in India. I would like to offer some explanation in this regard.

First, the purpose of disengaging oneself from society is not to cut ourselves off from material and physical needs of the body. If we do not obtain food, we risk dying. Hearing that certain Indian ascetics can live on one almond a year and such anecdotes are merely fables. The need to cut oneself off from people and the society means only to detach oneself from psychological interests and desires. Let's see how this works.

Assume that today I want to leave my family and seek shelter in the mountains. So, now that I am going to a mountain, do I take my spiritual and psychological attachments with me or not? Meaning, do I also take the "I?" Obviously I do. If I had let go of that, there would be no need to leave my current circumstances. Everywhere I go I take the "I" with me. I have only separated myself from society physically, but my mind is still attached by an invisible thread. If I do not have the ability to let go of this heavy burden (the "I") while living in the society, I won't have it in seclusion either.

In regard to the level of literacy, of course we should understand the common language of our own society. The simpler the language, the better. However, if you know more math and physics than I do, this would not affect self-realization. (Of course, if other suitable conditions are provided, a mathematical mind may reach awareness easier than an imbalanced or hallucinatory mind.)

In regards to being intelligent or unintelligent, I would say that this part of your question is futile. Suppose you are not very intelligent, can you do anything about it? The capacity of our intellect is what it is. We only need to avoid things that damage our minds and thus our level of intelligence.

*As a necessary introduction to self-realization, it seems to me that the most important factor is to realize the gravity of the problem.* We should feel with our whole being that we are trapped and how critical the liberation from that trap is. We should realize that our whole being is filled with fear and instability—fear of jeopardizing a bunch of "empty" values from which we have built an identity. Our being is partitioned, and we are constantly in conflict with ourselves and others. Our being is old and stale, and therefore we do not see life's freshness. *If we realize this, then we understand why all prophets, sages, and*

182

*philosophers consider self-realization the greatest and most im-*
*portant mission of our lives.*

Another basic point that we should recognize is that our current characteristics, habits, and behaviors have been developed in
the same order of growth as thought identity has. Now, we
should become aware of these characteristics and habits and
weaken them. For example, since childhood our inner connection
to existence has gradually been cut off and become dependent on
the opinions and judgments of others. As a result, we are disconnected from our roots. We live by external factors. We are still
continuing our childhood experiences.

For instance, as soon as my uncle would come for a visit, my
father would say to me, "Read your poems for your dear uncle."
And my uncle would say, "Bravo! What a smart boy." My mother would say, "My boy sends his greetings." And my aunt would
say, "What a polite boy." Now our lives are connected to a
bunch of words like "bravo," "smart" and "polite." Throughout
life most of our behaviors are a show in which we put our personality on display for the judgment of others.

Giving importance to external factors has caused us to stay
away from our inner essence. In order to get back to our true nature, we want to weaken the importance of these external factors.
I hope you do not misunderstand me. I am not saying to negate
external factors. I am not saying don't give any importance to
other human beings. I am saying to not give importance to their
empty and value-based judgments.

**Q:** *Doesn't "not giving importance to the value-based judg-*
*ments of others" cause social anarchy?*

**A:** No. I'm saying that love with its purity will rule our beings and all our relations. Our beings will find a spiritual and religious quality of purity, and there will not be any mischievous, selfish, or devilish qualities arising from the "I."

Our task is to weaken the dominance of the environment over ourselves so that we can return to our true nature and authenticity. The dominance of the environment that has been imposed upon us from childhood has changed us to hopeless and powerless human beings that can be controlled by external factors. Now, through direct understanding and insight, we should realize the invalidity of these externally dominant factors so that we can direct our attention to our inner beings. We should not be like a beggar who waits to see what judgments others might have about us. Any judgment that comes from thought identity has no validity. Therefore we should be unbiased and indifferent to such judgments. As Rumi says:

پیرو پیغمبرانی ره سپر
طعنه خلقان همه بادی شمر

*In footsteps of prophets carrying on the path,*
*Critique from others shall be taken as the wind.*

Another characteristic that has been imposed upon us from childhood is comparison, which contributes to the continuity of the "I." Do not compare yourself with others nor with your past. A mind that does not get involved in comparison cannot have an image of the "I."

Never blame yourself, and understand that any fear of blame is coming from ignorance. It is the fear of blame that forces us to constantly try to escape from ourselves and become disconnected from ourselves. We try to justify our actions so that we do not see their reality. If we do not look at ourselves through the lenses of guilt and self-recrimination, all that we are hiding from will be revealed to our minds. In other words, the moment that we stop blaming ourselves, the "I" ceases to exist. Not blaming ourselves means we have accepted ourselves as we are.

Since the judgments from others about our personalities are contradictory and uncertain, self-blame is inevitable. On the one hand, our lives may just be a pretense that is dependent on the judgments of others. On the other hand, there is not a moment that we do not blame ourselves for any of our acts based on this pretense, due to the contradictory quality of these acts.

Be aware that you blame yourself because there's an alien in the house. The whole personality that you are blaming yourself for is a false identity. Therefore, stop the habit of blaming yourself. By doing this you will see that the "I" no longer exists. It is from the fear of blame that you continue to insist on being something.

**Q:** *Are you saying that embellishment of our personalities and sense of value gets registered in the mind and creates a center that we call "I?" Well, if something is registered in the mind, how is it possible to have it disappear?*

**A:** From a physiological standpoint I do not know what kinds of relationships exist between "values" and the brain. Perhaps the word "registered" is not the exact correct expression; but in practice we can see that what is held in the mind might be removable. This of course depends on the extent to which we want to cling to the contents of the mind.

Let's look at this in a simple way. Let's assume a person on the street asks you if you have matches. A few moments later, I ask you what that person was asking for. You can easily remember that the person asked you whether you had matches. This indicates that the person's question has been registered in your mind. If it was not, if his question had not remained in your mind, certainly a few minutes or an hour later when I asked you about it, you wouldn't recall. But a year later or two or ten years later, is that person's question still fresh in your mind? Today, do you remember ten years ago when someone asked you whether you had matches? Obviously not. Hence, it is possible for something that is registered in the mind to fade and disappear. The reason that the disappearance of the "I" from the mind is so difficult is because we are sensitive to it, constantly anxious about it, constantly taking care of it, continuously trying to remember it because we want it to be alive and we believe that the "I" is what makes us exist. If we do not have any interest in its continuity, it will disappear.

**Q:** *Suppose we could reach this state of being that is devoid of an "I." By doing so, how can we then deal with people who have not reached this state, without feeling that they are incompatible with us?*

**A:** Every question about this that comes into our minds indicates some type of resistance. It exposes the fact that we are afraid to put down this heavy load. Therefore, we come up with excuses. We all assume that only one person can reach the state of not being identified with an "I"; and that person would be ourselves, and then as a liberated person, what are we supposed to do with the others?! It doesn't occur to us that *others* could be without thought identity, and how are *they* supposed to deal with unnatural and incompatible individuals such as we are!

But now let's assume that you really have realized yourself and I haven't. What problem could I possibly pose for you? Please bring precise examples, not hypothesis that would never occur or may rarely happen.

**Q:** *Suppose that you insult me or compromise my civil rights. Since there is no longer an "I" to defend, then I wouldn't feel the necessity of defending my rights at all, considering the characteristics that you have described!*

**A:** I think that you do not yet understand the condition and the reality of a person without thought identity. You can only guess or imagine this reality from a partial and incomplete context, not as a whole and connected experience.

For example, you may assume you are without thought identity; and you may also have ten million dollars and assume that now I want to steal some of your money. What are you supposed to do? You do not yet understand that the person without thought identity lives in love, and love is everything to that person. He or she does not need ten million dollars to fill an inner emptiness. This person's relationship with other human beings automatically comes from pure love that is not an act. Such a person would not be able to have ten million dollars in savings when their brothers and sisters are starving. Except for what is needed to sustain a real life, not a value-based life, this person does not save anything to be afraid of losing.

Your other question is that it may be possible that I insult you, and you wouldn't feel the urge to defend yourself. For instance, I may tell you that you are stupid, then what are you supposed to do?

As I said before, the center of gravity of the personality of a human being who is not separate from his or her authentic self has an existence rooted in their *whole* being, not in the judgment of others. External factors cannot disturb this person's spirituality with some borrowed words or toy with him/her.

Perhaps, you have noticed that when a child insults us we do not take it so personally or hold onto resentment. The reason is that a child cannot be a threatening factor to our sense of self-worth. If we can get all the borrowed values out of our minds and not be concerned with them, then anybody's insult would be seen as having the quality of a child's.

Apart from this, all the reactions, behaviors, and relationships of a person who lives with love are positive, useful, reasonable, and benevolent, not like our current situation, which is so often destructive and filled with disgust and bitterness. If I told you that you are stupid, I would most certainly be an ignorant man. I would not have much maturity from a moral and psychological perspective. Therefore, I would be deserving of your compassion and help more than your anger and disgust. If your reaction to me were brotherly and logical, instead of wrathful in an attempt to make me conscious of my ignorance, you might help me to see the error of my ways without the desire to punish me.

We have a strong tendency to explode due to having accumulated so much violence and anger in our beings. Basically, most of our moral behaviors and relations are built on violence. We are brought up in environments empty of kindness and compassion, and we have become accustomed to this. We do not know any other way to live but through aggression, noncooperation, and violence. And it is interesting that we equate aggression with having a strong personality. Whereas the truth is that at a deep and fundamental level, we are filled with feelings of fear, helplessness, and distrust in ourselves or anyone else. And all these violent and childish tendencies are to cover that deep sense of fear and helplessness.

An authentic human being is not afraid of others who are embroiled in thought identity, and this person is very relational with others. Fears and weaknesses are the properties of those who are caught in thought identity. We are the ones that create problems for each other. We are the ones who are wounded and crying out with the tiniest of touch from others. We are the ones with flimsy straw-like structures as our spiritual basis, built on the water, blown away with the smallest breeze. An authentic human being is like a mountain, sturdy and stable yet gentle.

Related to your question, another of the characteristics of active thought is that it imposes on our lives an ongoing quality of incompleteness, like there's always unfinished business. We never experience a whole and complete relationship with life and its circumstances. Any one of our present relations is connected to hundreds of previous relations. For every relation we create a file in our minds that we link to a previous relation or the next relation.

For instance, you may ask to borrow some money from me. First I refer to the file stored in my mind that has something to do with you from past events. Then I ask myself if this is the same person that last year lent me some money or not? Is this the same person that last week showed me respect or not? Has this person listened to my talks with a sense of appreciation or negative judgment? Does this person look like someone that I do or do not like—and hundreds of such thoughts that may enter my mind?

Therefore, I am not present to your current situation with an open mind. Rather, my attitude toward you is like a mental thread linked to past relations. We hold on to all these mental files that we have kept about our relationships with others, and from our attachment to the past continue to live second-hand lives. And goodness knows how much energy we waste in protecting these files! In almost any present relation, all the previous files that mostly contradict each other are in conflict within our minds. And one of the reasons for our underlying anxiety and agitation are these very conflicts.

Have you noticed how often you sleep freely, deeply, and calmly? Whether in sleep or in wakefulness the mind's job is to always be dealing with these mental files that we are dependent on, the files that have remained incomplete and will never be finished. Our minds have become places for all these little thoughts that are constantly buzzing and whispering about those files.

Every relation of a human being whose existence is not ruled by thought identity is a new, complete, and independent relation. Any decision—except regarding physical and concrete matters—happens without relating the current matter to the prior mater or the next matter. Every encounter with life's circumstances is whole and complete. The mind does connect every new relation by an invisible thread to the past.

Say, for instance, someone insults you. You have displayed a specific reaction, whether rough or gentle, and it is over. You do not carry the current circumstances with you, even into the sleep state and constantly review the same problem over and over. At night, when you are sleeping, you do have any give-and-take with the world or other people. In the morning, when you wake up, you begin a fresh relationship with the world and everyone you encounter throughout your day. In this way, life is new for you, not the old and dead existence of thought identity.

The necessity of determination is only relevant to the spiritual aspects of our lives. What is hidden by the power of free will is that our relationship with life is already complete and absolute in every moment; and thus there is no psychological give-and-take with life.

As I said, one of our difficulties is that we consider our existence as an "I" to be sound criterion for examination and judgment. However, who we believe ourselves to be as this "I" is out of harmony with our true nature and distorted in its reasoning. If our true nature were realized, our intellect and logic would not be altered and confused, and instead they could be in the service of our nature. Goodness knows what a beautiful creature could be built from the cooperation of these two. The problem is that we have ruined both. Neither has our nature kept its authenticity, nor has our intellect acted correctly.

**Q:** *I have two questions: What is the role of free will in the possibility of realizing our true nature? And what is the cause for any lack of free will? Why do some have stronger wills than others?*

**A:** As mentioned in a previous chapter, the type of will you are referring to is one of thought identity's tools and is at its service. Therefore, it does not have any role in self-realization. In self-realization, there are no ideas about vanquishing the self because that self no longer exists, whereas the will is like a belt that clamps pieces of the "self" together and keeps it strong.

Your second question is about the cause for lack of will. We know that we are not just one person. If we were to look at ourselves carefully, we would pick a hundred different names for ourselves. Every moment we put on a different mask and change the face that we present to the world. One moment I imagine myself to be a kind ascetic. The next moment I may imagine myself as Napoleon. Maybe the following moment I label myself a spiritual person, and in another moment I may see myself as a clever man. For one moment I am rough and filled with condemnation; the next moment I am gentle and forgiving. Our beings have been partitioned amongst the different "Is," each one with a different form, color, goal, and desire. Every moment one of the "Is" becomes dominant over one's being and declares itself to be the representative of the rest of the "Is," and acts as their proxy, even when the act of the dominant "I" is not approved of by the other "Is."

Let's assume a hundred people live in a city with different names such as Mike, David, Carol, John, etc. For a moment Mike becomes the ruler of the town and wants to manage the other three's affairs; the next moment David, Carol, and John want to do the same thing. It happens that David does not like Mike's decisions, and Mike and Carol do not like David's decisions. As a result, there won't be harmony in this town. The people's affairs will not progress in an orderly manner, fluid and without hindrance.

Our beings are like this city. For example, I may be addicted to cigarettes, and I decide to quit smoking tomorrow. But I see that following days and months I continue to smoke. The reason for this is that the "I" who desires to smoke (suppose Mike), and the "I" who desires to stop smoking (suppose David), and the "I" who should execute this decision (suppose John), are not the same. Mike likes smoking, but David does not like it. When David is ruling, he decides to quit; whereas the next moment he is not ruling and Mike is. In fact, the problem of the lack of will is the result of different "Is" that do not listen to each other and at the same time contradict each other.

Why do some decide to quit smoking and they can but others cannot? In many cases, the "will" is not an issue and has nothing to do with the problem, rather it is the power and tension of the "Is" that pushes us to one side or the other. However, in some cases, besides the degree of power of the different "Is," the will itself has a role as a separate and independent power. In other words, many of the "servants" who serve the structure of thought identity, in addition to having their own specific duty as independent "Is," are also the building blocks of that structure. Like people of a country, each person is a member of the country and also has their specific duties within the organization of that country's society. The will, besides having the supplementary role of arbitrator and monitor, has its own independent "I." Those who have a stronger will than others are those whose will, besides having a specific duty, is also one of the important "Is" that form the structure of their identity. In this way, the will as an independent "I" has power and dominance, and hence finds a more magnificent manifestation.

I should also explain that when the will acts as an independent "I," its main goal is to protect its own survival, over and above whatever action it accomplishes. When you quit smoking with the power of the will (the will that acts as an independent "I"), the protection and subsistence of the I-with-a-will is more important than the actual quitting. There are some people who, after attempting to accomplish a specific goal, realize that the effort is futile; however they do not dare leave the job for fear of that I-with-a-will.

**Q:** *Aren't those who live in civilized societies and modern metropolises even more prone to getting caught up in the trap of the "I?"*

**A:** There is no real relationship between those two. It is only possible that the type of "Is" differ from each other.

Some time ago I went to visit some gypsies in one of the villages in Shiraz. After just a few minutes the gypsy chief said to me, "Do you know that we are descendants of Kaveh The Blacksmith?" (A mythical figure in Persian mythology who led a popular uprising against the ruthless ruler, Zahhak.) Well, could any life be simpler than the nomadic lifestyle and still have this much arrogance?!

**Q:** *Doesn't the expression, "We are descendants of Kaveh The Blacksmith," indicate the gypsies' deprivation of comfort and pleasure?*

**A:** It is completely the reverse. The "I" itself is the cause of feelings of deprivation and disappointment. The ambiguous perception the gypsy may have of himself and the world might result in the belief: "Look how mean life treats the descendants of Kaveh The Blacksmith, who now live in a dry desert with their only skill the making of some cheap handicraft."

Unfortunately, all human beings imagine themselves as the descendants of Kaveh The Blacksmith. And all of our deprivations and our feelings of disappointment, envy, discontent, and the demands put on us from the world and the people of the world are rooted in this same kind of imagination. Our whole lives may be spent with a feeling of envy that compels us to reach the position of Kaveh The Blacksmith. Our whole lives may be a struggle between what we are and what we should become, between a simple handicraft maker that is our present reality and reaching for an idealistic image like Kaveh The Blacksmith. Any idealistic image from the perspective of not being fulfilled is a mirage.

# CHAPTER TEN

# ARE YOU REALLY SERIOUS?

B efore we continue our discussion of the previous chapters, there are a few points that I need to bring to your attention. The first is that our purpose for gathering to discuss different subjects is not to help each other gain more knowledge. *Our aim is to help each other become aware. Being aware is different from filling the mind with knowledge. Our desire is to know ourselves practically, not to store more knowledge about ourselves in our memories. Practicing and fully embodying our true nature is more than "knowing" it.* We have stored thousands of theories and hypothesis in our mental repositories without acting in accordance with a single one of them. If we only acted on the contents of one of these theories, meaning to be a part of that content, it would be a finished business. I hope that you do not treat this subject as yet another mental concept.

Let's not deceive ourselves by constantly going after more knowledge. Gaining knowledge is only of value for selling something or for bragging. Self-realization is about something entirely different. Switching from one system to another is no use to us here. Our problem is not a system. *Our problem is not wanting the truth enough.* Our task here is to increase our yearning, not gain more knowledge. Increase in yearning is related to the present, not to tomorrow or the future. Do not deceive yourself with tomorrow's mirage. Whatever will be here tomorrow is already here today. What could be in tomorrow that does not already exist in the here and now?

This is a serious matter. Let us become more attentive in life about what we say, what we listen to, and in general to contemplate all circumstances of life.

We have heard it said in every religion and philosophy of morals that self-realization is the ultimate jewel. We have heard that if you want to know God, know yourself first. So, if we are not paying attention to self-realization, what kind of people might we be? Why aren't we interested in self-realization? Shouldn't self-realization have at least as much importance as a material possession or a petty entertainment? Oh I wish we could understand that life has a meaning deeper than all these games around us!

The other important thing to understand is that self-realization is not just for a specific individual or group. A man who does not know himself, knows nothing really. As long as the mind is busy with the "self," it is unable to see reality. Thought arises from a self-created center and only knows that center, as thought activity is only in the domain of that center. Initially, the brain, meaning in its original and healthy state, is a center of communications with the body and the world, but when it becomes a center for the "I," it turns out as an exclusive means in the service of the "I," and sees all life circumstances in relation to the "I," not as they are. Basically, the mind gets so captivated by the "I" that it cannot pay attention to anything other than that center.

The person who does not know himself/herself is an immature person. This person could be used as a pawn for propaganda. A mind that is caught up in the "I" is a blind mind, an obscured mind that cannot see everything clearly. I hope we all understand the importance of this problem.

One of the criticisms of new systems of spirituality, or ideologies such as psychoanalysis and psychology, is that they have made the topic of self-realization superficial and limited. The subjects of these systems are only those individuals who exhibit abnormal behaviors in their specific societies; and the defined criteria for abnormality are superficial, limited, and conventional.

For example, in the specific society where a psychologist resides, if most individuals are perky, tough, selfish, unkind or even deceivers and charlatans, and one person is not like the rest, that person may not be considered normal according to others' behavioral patterns, and he may need to go to a psychologist for therapy. That's what I mean by a superficial and limited criterion.

In the old ideologies and traditions, the criteria were wide open and extensive; and self-realization basically had a much deeper and more fundamental meaning than just touching upon and touching up a person's personality. The criteria for being abnormal were not due to lack of adaptation to specific social norms. Rather, they were mostly based on authentic human values such as love, consciousness, kindness, human virtue, the harmony of human relationships, and the harmony of humans with the environment, not a specific society or specific individuals.

The purpose of this explanation is to illustrate that even if we appear completely normal in a given society, we still need self-realization. If we look at the criteria for being abnormal from a broader perspective, we see that no matter which social group we are a part of, whether religious or secular, theist or atheist, materialist or non-materialist, we need self-realization. It is said, "To know yourself is to know God." We could also say to know yourself so that you are free of an empty life. Know yourself so you can see and experience life freshly in every moment. Know yourself so you become conscious and free. Know yourself so you can get out of the trap set by the "I," and be free from thousands of problems and suffering. Then if you do not believe in God, at least know yourself for the sake of eliminating these problems.

Understand that I do not claim all I talk about is correct, or subjects related to self-realization would be limited to only the topics I have covered in this book. If you accept the two principles that firstly, we are living with a lot of unnecessary and aggravating problems and suffering, and secondly that the cause of all this suffering is a delusional and borrowed entity called the "I," then you will find the ways to fight it yourself. Do not just rely on my words. Perhaps I may be mistaken in the depiction of this phenomenon, the cause of its creation, and how to get rid of it. You need to examine and understand all these in your own right. So, in any way that you are able, please start the work.

# ARE YOU REALLY SERIOUS?

\*\*\*

**Q:** *In my opinion what you are talking about is clear, acceptable, and mentally digestible.* But tomorrow I may go to another meeting and participate in another discussion, and I may hear talks contradictory to yours, which may also seem to be correct. Next comes the mental argument, who is right and who is wrong?

**A:** I think whoever is behind a microphone is right! Now that I have the microphone before me, I am right! If the next moment the microphone is before you, then you would be right. Recognize that this microphone metaphor may have many forms.

A few days ago I was attending a memorial service. As soon as the service was over, the crowd rushed to the speaker (apparently he was a famous fellow) to kiss his hand. An old guy with a limp reached him and kissed his hand. While returning to his seat, he asked me, "Who is that person?" In this case, the large crowd rushing to kiss the man's hand had the quality of a microphone. And we constantly move from one position to another by hearing from different kinds of microphones. We have become human beings who are heavily under the influence of propaganda. The "mold" of thought identity that we have been talking about is, in fact, the result of propaganda imposed on our minds. As long as this mold exists in us, and rules our view and our relationships, discerning true and false, discerning right and wrong, would be difficult. Whenever we reject or accept something, it is in fact the mold that has rejected or accepted. We can only understand something consciously and freely when we look without the interference of the mold.

# THE POWER OF NO THOUGHT

**Q:** *Why is it that when man knows himself he will know God as well? What is the relation between the "self" and God?*

**A:** First let's look at how we define God. Simply, God is defined as an indescribable essence with three basic characteristics: beyond matter, outside of time, and outside of space. While holding this definition, let's go back to the "I."

The characteristics of the "I" are completely the reverse. First of all, the creator of this phenomenon is thought and thought is rooted in matter. Secondly, thought is rooted in and has its continuity in time. Thirdly, thought is bound to dimensions within space (although hypothetical dimensions.) A thought that has been formed from the "I," no matter how far it flies, will be bound and halted at some point. The movement of such thought is inside a boundary, in the domain of known matters. Thought arises from the "I" and goes back to the "I." Therefore it is limited to a boundary. If these three characteristics were taken away from the mind, the "I" would vanish and the mind would become disengaged from the restrictions of time and space. It would automatically be connected to infinity, outside of time and outside of space.

Rumi describes this concept beautifully in an allegorical story in the Masnavi. The story is about how a nomad carried a jug of rainwater from the midst of the desert as a gift to the commander of Baghdad who lived on the shores of the Tigris River. This was done in the belief that the town was suffering from a shortage of water. He wants to tell us that whatever we know as known is so limited. The contents of our minds have formed the "I" and these contents and this "I" are what separate us from the infinite ocean of unity.

202

# ARE YOU REALLY SERIOUS?

چیست آن کوزه؟ تن محصور ما
اندر آن آب حواس شور ما
ای خداوند این خم و کوزه مرا
در پذیر از فضل الله اشتری
تا شود زین کوزه منفذ سوی بحر
تا بگیرد کوزه ما خوی بحر
تا چو هدیه پیش سلطانش بری
پاک بیند باشدش شه مشتری
بی نهایت گردد آبش بعد از آن
پر شود از کوزه ما صد جهان
ای که اندر چشمه شور است جات
تو چه دانی شط و جیحون و فرات
ای تو نارسته از این فانی رباط
تو چه دانی محو و سکر و انبساط

*What is that jar? Our bodily vessel,*
*In its water our salty senses nestle.*

*O Lord, accept this curved jug of mine,*
*In place, return the high blessing thine.*

*That the mouth of the jar leads to the sea,*
*That my jar may obtain the quality of the sea.*

*So if you take it to the king as a gift,*
*The King would see it as pure and would be a buyer.*

*After that, its water will become without limit,*
*A hundred worlds will be filled from my jug.*

# THE POWER OF NO THOUGHT

*O those whose abode is in the briny spring,*
*How could you know about the sea and the Jaihoon And the*
*Euphrates?*

*O you who have not run out of this mortal borough,*
*How could you know the meaning of self-annihilation And*
*intoxication and ecstasy?*

Again Rumi, in another passage in the same context, says:

آن سبوی آب، دانش های ماست
وآن خلیفه دجله علم خداست
آن عرب باری بدان معذور بود
کو ز دجله غافل و بس دور بود
آن سبوی تنگ پر ناموس و رنگ
شد حجاب بحر، زن آنرا به سنگ
نه سبو پیدا در این حالت نه آب
خوش ببین، والله اعلم باالصواب

*That vessel of water is our collection of knowledge,*
*And that King is God's River of knowledge.*

*The nomad was forgivable for that,*
*As he was unaware of the River and so far away from it.*

*That tight vessel full of virtues and colors,*
*Blocked the River, smash it on a rock.*

# ARE YOU REALLY SERIOUS?

*In this state neither the vessel is manifest nor the water,*
*Consider well, and God knows best what is right.*

I don't think that this concept could have been described more beautifully and more eloquently than this. And what kind of human beings are we that we do not contemplate and recognize these messages! We presume that Rumi only wanted to say some verses that we would enjoy and make a song out of. I wish we could all see that Rumi's finger is pointing to the tiny jug of our brains and saying to us, "Hey brother! Yes, I'm calling you, you! Throw away the salty and vain content of your jug (brain)! I am dying for a bit of correct understanding!"

Another subject I'd like to bring up is that we agreed to discuss problems, questions, and subjects that could help us somehow in knowing our true nature. For example, you may ask what is the truth, what is love, what are the states and qualities of man without the "I," and so on. Bringing up any other question is useless because your motive is to know about the end of the path, whereas our problem is the beginning of the path. You are talking about *there*, whereas I am talking about *here*. We are here, not there. We do not know of there. When we ask someone else what is love or the truth, it is obvious that we do not know those qualities for ourselves; we are not in touch with the essence of these qualities. If we were, we would not ask. And not being in touch with these qualities indicates that there are obstacles, a veil, and rather than God, what we want to know about is the obstacles and the veil. So let's examine what is the veil and how we can remove it. If the veil is gone, you will see what love or truth is. There will be no need for someone to describe it for you.

As long as the veil is in place, how does the description of the truth help you?!

**Q:** *In the previous discussions you negated the search. In my opinion, negating the search is like negating the hope and the goal. When we are not searching for anything, when we have no goal, then neither do we have hope of relief from life's problems. Are we just to accept life as it is with all its problems? That would seem like a petrified and static life.*

**A:** Let's go beyond words and see what the reality of search is, or the lack of a search. For example, we are in a prison and we hear that on the other side of the prison's wall is a beautiful forest. I am not saying it is not necessary to free ourselves from the prison and reach the forest. Reaching the forest, meaning becoming free, is your natural right. I am only saying that instead of thinking about the forest; think about the prison. That does not mean to stay in the prison. I am saying to examine and know the prison itself! When you become familiar with what is happening in your own being's prison, you will see that this prison is self-made. Its walls are formed by your delusional thoughts. When the mind stops its delusions, you have entered the forest. More precisely, when the mind stops its delusional thinking, wherever you are, so is the beautiful forest. Searching for yourself outside the forest while you're already in the forest will make no sense, and therefore you are no longer "reaching."

**Q:** *Aren't imagining the forest and having enthusiasm and earnestness strong motives for getting out of the prison?*

**A:** No. Now you must forget about the forest example because you have already created the dualistic belief that you are here and the forest is out there somewhere. Do not think that you are physically in San Quentin and a few miles farther behind the walls of the prison lies a forest. The forest I am speaking of is all of life. This forest is already attached to you, but you separate yourself from it by a wall of delusion. Therefore, any activity of searching or any thought of reaching the forest is meaningless. Wherever you are, there also is the forest. Just remove the division in your mind and be in the forest.

Presently you are living in the ocean of existence; but you hold yourself inside a jug by your own mind activity. And this imaginary mental jug is all that separates you from the ocean. Be in union with the ocean.

Additionally, thinking about the forest and having enthusiasm for reaching the forest are not valid motives for getting out of the prison. It is completely the reverse. The only things that might result from thinking about the forest are envious hopes and wishes. And in that wishful thinking is a fundamentally crushing hidden conflict—the conflict between the prison and the forest.

We have felt stuck in this conflict, and trying to resolve this conflict is wasting all our energy. If we remove the image of forest from our minds, the result is freedom from conflict and conservation of energy. A mind that is not in conflict has a calm, untroubled, and fearless quality. And such a quality of the mind can see everything clearly.

Apart from this, having an image in our minds of a forest out there somewhere hinders our ability to see and know the prison holistically. Half of the mind may be thinking about the forest while the other half is thinking about other things. In addition, the forest that we imagine and are searching for is a self-made mirage that itself has the substance of a prison, and all the while we are calling it a forest.

By way of analogy, the prison that I am in is an image like "self-pity." The forest that I am searching for is an image like "self-esteem." This image is a reaction to the image of self-pity, and it also has the delusional characteristic of self-pity even though I may be imagining it differently. Naturally there is a quality different from self-pity beyond my imagination, but I do not know that quality. I can only reach that quality beyond my imagination when my mind is freed from all its present contents, meaning from the delusions of prison and forest, self-pity and self-esteem.

Emptying the mind of its contents does not mean emptying the mind from the quality of attention, which is the innate function of thought.

**Q:** *How can we keep the true knowledge, and empty the other contents that belong to the "I"? How does this refinement and separation happen?*

**A:** When the mind only looks at life and its circumstances without personal interpretation, the refinement happens automatically.

**Q:** *Once the "I" is vanquished and nothing remains but our innate spirituality, will that continue to grow and evolve? And is its growth in our control or does it happen automatically? Secondly, is the essence of our spirituality the same for everyone or does it vary from person to person?*

**A:** Both questions are futile in that answering them won't help us in any way. Go ahead and vanquish thought identity and then see. If the innate spirituality wants to grow more, let it grow, and if it grows automatically and your will cannot influence it, what can you do about it? If the growth and evolution are part of its essence, whether you want it or not, it will grow and evolve automatically. If it is not capable of growing more, what can you do about it?

Your question is something akin to having your feet bound and then questioning, if your feet were not tied up could you run thirty miles per hour. And I would respond that it would not be possible, because if your feet were bound you couldn't even run ten miles per hour. The discussion is futile. If the feet were free to run there would be no need for discussion. We could practically see at what speed we can run, or even run at all.

For now, you and I are slaves to an inauthentic phenomenon called "I." So let's cut off its dominance and live as our authentic self. Once we realize the authentic self, we'll see whether it continues to grow, whether any of it is under our control. Why do you want to know the results of a situation that has not yet occurred?

Your second question is futile as well. Whether the essence of our spirituality is the same for each of us. What is it that you hope to conclude? What do you want to get out of it? Is the essence of another's spirituality our business? Anyway, if you think resolving this question would have a benefit, Rumi has already clearly addressed it:

چون شناسد جان من جان تو را

یاد آرد اتحاد ماجرا

موسی و هارون شوند اندر زمین

مختلط خوش همچو شیر و انگبین

*When my soul sees your soul,*
*It recalls the secret of us once whole.*

*On the Earth, they'll be like Moses and Aaron,*
*Joyfully mixed like milk and honey on this barren.*

And again in another verse he writes:

چونکه بی رنگی اسیر رنگ شد

موسی با موسی در جنگ شد

چون به بی رنگی رسی کان داشتی

موسی و فرعون دارند آشتی

*Those free of color, enslaved by color in deceit,*
*Sent Moses upon Moses into war and defeat.*

*Shed your color; be as you were of old,*
*Moses and Pharaoh into friendship bold.*

The contents of these points emphasize unity and oneness as the core of human spirituality, or more precisely, they indicate the unity that results from our innate oneness.

**Q:** *Doesn't knowing others help us to know ourselves?*

**A:** First of all, considering the existence of thought identity, knowing others is impossible. We know others through our thought identities. Secondly, knowing others is not necessary, and I'll expand upon this a little later on. Perhaps if we change the question to, "Why do we need and insist upon knowing others?" it would be more useful.

# ARE YOU REALLY SERIOUS?

In my opinion the reason that we are interested in knowing others is fear. It seems as though we are incredibly afraid of each other. Each one of us might be a dangerous factor for the other by means of words, behavior, and even with silence, which can completely confuse and stir up each other's identity. Considering how our identities are dear to us, and how our psychological existences dependent upon our identities, it is not hard to imagine how we might fear each other.

However, we usually hide our fears due to two basic reasons, and we even stay unaware of the depths and severity of our fear. The first reason is that we consider fear to be weak and degrading. Secondly, we think if our rivals know about our fears, they can target us and hurt us. Therefore, we usually put on a mask of control and composure and pretend we are not afraid. We are rough and demanding in our relationships, we guard ourselves by pretending to have strong personalities, we try to get ahead of the others, and a thousand other things we might do to cover up our fears.

One of the ways to be immune to harassment from others is to know them. I think that if I know you better, meaning I know this "potentially dangerous being," I can safeguard myself against your harassment, get along with and tolerate you better. I try to learn about your sensitive and weak points that I myself can use as targets. I also want to know your strong points so that I can defend myself if need be or neutralize their effects. Regardless, whatever our strategies may be, it seems to me that the most important reason for our interest in knowing others is fear.

The other reason we want to know others is our desire to escape from ourselves. In order to get away from my own con-

211

flicts, insecurities, and fears, I ignore myself and focus on you instead. Many of us do this, of course without being aware of it. And this is one of thought's deceits to keep us away from our true selves. If I imagine I know you, I imagine I know myself.

But let's investigate this issue from a different angle. If we change our motives and perspectives for knowing others, I think we can find an important benefit in it.

In spite of being alien to ourselves and all our strivings and excuses for not seeing our own internal weaknesses, from another corner of our minds we are witnessing everything that we perceive and experience. However, we usually prefer to close our eyes to what we see rather than be aware of how unstable we human beings are, and how we are enslaved to our inner conflicts, fears, and sensitivities. And neither do we see such weaknesses and sensitivities in others because that might bring us closer to having to see our own, and so we often isolate ourselves from others. Secondly, we show a different image of ourselves to others, rather than who we really are, by putting on different masks and shows of pretense and playing different games. Therefore each one of us imagines that others are what they show. I pretend to be calm in spite of my inner insecurity and restlessness, I show off how my life is full of happiness and satisfaction, and I cover my uncertainties and fears by putting on a mask of courage and high self-esteem, and do not let you see how fragile and filled with pain I truly am inside. As a result, your own self-pity and low self-esteem causes you to feel even more separate from me and others. Our situation is like two soldiers with empty guns trained on each other. Each one thinks the other one's gun is loaded and thus we are both afraid. We see

212

ourselves as weak when compared to the other, whom we may consider powerful and capable. We usually think that others can do what we cannot; others live easy lives and we live with pain and sorrow. It is obvious that such views and imagination create a lot of problems in our relationships. When I perceive that I am weak and you are strong, clearly I will have fear of you, feel less than you, feel envious of you, and be filled with resentment toward you, along with a host of other problems. Then I struggle to whitewash those problems by coming up with all kinds of excuses.

Now, if you and I, meaning the two soldiers confronting each other, realized the reality that the other one is in the same situation we are, and we are each putting on a pretense of power, our views would be completely changed towards each other. Then the daring acts of one person (which in fact are only a cover up for fear,) and the so-called weakness of the other person, would be no more. When there is no fear, no self-pity, and no hatred within either of us, our relationship has a completely different quality than a relationship that is ruled by fear and hatred. From this reality, we can empathize with our brothers and sisters and not consider them to be dangerous monsters. Understanding the truth that the situation of others is really no better than our own makes us more at ease in our relationships.

When we feel comfortable and safe in our relationships with others, we find more opportunity to be at peace within ourselves, to pay attention to what is going on inside us, to inquire into our beings and become more familiar with ourselves. If our attention is taken up by fear of others and protecting ourselves from others becomes what is most important, then we do not find the opportunity to come to ourselves, to spend time with ourselves in silence, and to see who we are and how quickly our lives are passing us by. Our minds are constantly worrying about how to deal with others.

If we pay close attention to our thought processes, we can see just how much of the time we are having arguments with others in our minds and constantly worrying about an imaginary danger from others. We can see just how often our attention is taken up with means of comparing ourselves to others and struggling to come up with schemes to challenge others. Whereas if others lose their importance as something dangerous to us, we can come home to ourselves, meaning that we can pay attention to ourselves and get to know ourselves better. And please note that what I mean by "paying attention to the self" is different from our usual self-centered activities.

**Q:** *What is the usefulness of dream interpretation in self-realization? As you know, psychology recognizes dreaming as one of the important aspects of our existence and gives considerable importance to dream interpretation and knowledge. What is your opinion in this regard?*

**A:** In order to clarify this subject we need to first be clear on another subject, which is that of the unconscious self. Dreams and the unconscious are closely related.

By "unconscious" we are referring to the existence of feelings, inclinations, needs, motives, wishes, sensitivities, fears, weaknesses, and generally all characteristics that a person is not conscious of that exist as a kind of "shadow" self. This means that the entity we consider as the "I" is a mixture of different psychological qualities, some of which we are conscious of and some of which we are not conscious of, without having a clear border between these two realms. Dreams are filled with the content of the unconscious self and so psychoanalysis pays attention to our dreams.

Another aspect of the unconscious self is the content of the unknown outside the domain of thought identity; meaning, qualities that are presently unknown to us. However, applying the word "self" or "I" to the unconscious self is not correct. Regardless, this aspect of self is outside the purposes of our discussion here, therefore let's not get into it.

The unconscious self that we are concerned with is an entity within the domain of thought. Isn't thought the creator of the whole identity called the "I?" Considering this, how can we say that thought has created an entity that it is unconscious of? Whatever is in the domain of thought is also in the domain of the known. What we consider "self" is not a thing outside and separate from thought. The self and thought are one and the same.

Now let's look at the subject of the unconscious self from the perspective that thought creates an entity in which some of its elements and tendrils have conflict and disharmony with others. And the unconscious self is about thought being blind to and ignoring these disharmonies. In other words, the unconscious self is the result of conflict. Thought identity, due to its structure, has to protect itself by always ignoring those conflicting aspects of its structure and pretends not to know about them. And we call this "unconsciousness," yet it is a deliberate unconsciousness.

Now, let's investigate what correlation dreams have to the unconscious self. In regard to dreams, just as with the unconscious self, we also need to look at the two types of dreams. One type are those dreams that arise from our unknown being and bring messages; the other type are those dreams that arise from the unconscious self of our known being, in other words from the domain of thought and thought identity.

As far as I know, the subject of dream interpretation in psychoanalysis refers to the latter type of dreams. Psychoanalysts say that the unconscious self, due to the mind's strong censorship during wakefulness, does not have opportunity to manifest. In sleep, however, since the power of censorship weakens, unconscious material can emerge from the mind and become conscious in the form of a dream, and dreaming is the result of this process. Thus, a dream is in fact a symbolic and complex duplicate of the hidden or unconscious self. Consequently, if we understand the meaning of the symbols and complex messages that come from the unconscious self, we can then become more familiar with the unconscious part of ourselves and so more familiar with ourselves. *As I said earlier, the unconscious self forms a big part of the self; and dreams are signs that can guide us and illumine the dark, less conscious corners of the self.*

Now let's see how much of this supposition is correct and how much is incorrect. I think it is correct that dreams are basically a symbolic and complex form of the unconscious self. It is also correct that we can receive messages of the unconscious by interpreting and understanding our dreams. But let's consider the use of this task, because a subject can be right but not necessarily useful.

What is the ultimate goal and purpose of analysis, dream interpretation, "free association" (a technique that is used in psychoanalysis), hypnotism, and such therapeutic modalities? Certainly these are a means, not the goal. The ultimate goal of all these methods is that they should be in service to self-realization; and that knowledge should have the aim of dissolving the false or egoic self that is constructed by thought. Otherwise, no useful knowledge has been obtained.

Do you remember the analogy of ghosts or the shadow self mentioned earlier? I gave the example that my mind, due to some flaws, imagines there are ghosts in this room. The only way I can tell that my mind has understood its mistake is if it has no further images of ghosts. Otherwise, any reasoning or method, however logical and scientific, would ultimately be useless.

Now let's examine whether the dream interpretation, no matter how accurate it might be, would get us to the ultimate result, meaning the dissolution of the "I."

Let's say I want to know my unconscious self by interpreting my dreams; that is, to know some aspect of an entity my mind has deliberately kept in the dark, in an unknown state, and that the continuance of this mind is the cause for keeping these aspects unconscious. In this case, isn't the work we're calling "self-realization" more like self-deceit? The so-called unconscious self is not a thing that has been hiding in some corners of our minds and then attempts to enter our consciousness during sleep. The unconscious self is in fact a collection of ill-matched experiences that the ideal structure of thought identity cannot cope with and so deliberately tries to be aware of. Then does it make sense that thought wants to keep something in the dark and then at the same time wants to bring it out of obscurity?

THE POWER OF NO THOUGHT

You might interpret my dreams accurately, but what is the ultimate result of this work? The result is that I admire you for your knowledge and experience in interpreting dreams, and then by picking up some incoherent information that active thought is receiving for the "I," I imagine that I now know myself.

**Q:** *Might the conscious self want to know the unconscious self?*

**A:** Let us not get twisted up in words and distracted from the main point. Aren't both the conscious self and the unconscious self in the domain of the active thought? The quality of thinking that arises from the identity or the self, whether it is the conscious self or the unconscious self, it is essentially an image and a delusion. And obviously using delusional thoughts as a means of knowledge is meaningless.

Suppose a person's mind is buried in prejudice and ignorance. Such a person thinks that he/she knows the truth of certain situation; but what is perceived by such an ignorant mind is not the truth even if the person imagines it as the truth. This would be truth within the framework of ignorance. It may be possible for me to interpret my dreams accurately and correctly, but this "accuracy" and "correctness" are in the framework of active thought, not the objective truth. This accuracy and correctness in terms of a person's specific identity structure may seem accurate and correct, but since the whole thought identity is managing the task of interpretation, with its inherent quality of ignorance, any perception gained this way is also ignorance.

Let's examine this matter from a different angle. When you or I say "I know myself or I am getting to know myself," we should ask ourselves this important question: who is this "I?"

218

Who or what is the factor that has known or is getting to know the "I?" Are these two different entities? Is this anything different from thought knowing thought? Certainly, both are comprised of thought. In this case, can thought know itself? Are thought that is the subject of examination and thought that tries to know two different thoughts from two different thought categories or are they the same? You may say that "passive thought" is the element that knows, and "active thought," meaning the "I," is the subject of that knowing. In this case thought is coming from two different branches. I accept this assumption on the condition that we actually conduct our lives this way. That is, we actually use passive thought as the one that seeks self-realization. Let's see whether we can practically approach it this way?

Suppose I want to know myself through interpretation of my dreams or psychoanalysis or any other way. I am also aware that thought, the means of knowing the self, does not have the same substance as the self. If it did, then any knowledge gained is certainly negated and thought is merely playing with itself. So, as we follow this process together in our quest to know the self, thought should be in a "passive" quality. As we have agreed on this assumption, let's actually play out this scenario in our minds.

Now, let's suppose that for half an hour we will focus our attention to the action of "knowing ourselves." Remember our agreement is that first we should devise the means of self-knowledge or the factor that will be doing the act of learning. Also we've agreed that this instrument of learning is the quality of thought that we call passive thought. Okay, let's practice now.

**Q:** *If we could create a passive quality in our minds for half an hour, that means during this time our thought cannot be en-*

*gaged in active thought, which means that during this time thought has become free of the "I." Therefore there can be no target of knowing for passive thought.*

**A:** That is completely correct. Realizing this truth indicates the end of the problem. It creates a trap for the "I" to become annihilated in. Is this clear for everyone?

We have now become aware that every movement of the active thought is like a game of the "I" with the "I." This means that active thought cannot work on itself and know itself. If it tries, it will in fact back itself into a dead end and chase its own tail. What result can be obtained from understanding this truth? *Try to feel this matter with the depth of your own being. The mind has reached an extent of awareness in which it can see that any struggle, any jumping up and down (meaning active thinking), would only exacerbate the problem.* In this case what happens to the mind? Obviously, it stops its struggle and striving and becomes calm. This calmness means the end of the problem.

**Q:** *For whom is this awareness and understanding? Isn't it for active thought?*

**A:** *No. We should be clear that not all of our understandings are obtained by active thinking.* Active thought obtains its information from the "I" and is produced by the "I." For instance, when you say the total length of two sides of a triangle is longer than the remaining side, my mind perceives and accepts this as a truth without interference from the "I."

**Q:** *In my opinion, it is an understandable truth that any understanding obtained by active thought is only a game of thought with thought. But this is a problem for me because I can observe that awareness of some individuals in relation to their self is* *more than others, though they also live in the domain of thought identity and active thought. How do you explain?*

**A:** Those individuals who seem to have a clearer understanding of their "selves" and have more knowledge and information in this regard usually are able to talk more clearly about the self. But this is not to say that their minds are really any clearer than others in relation to the self. As I pointed out, awareness is still present when the "self" has simultaneously departed the mind. Otherwise, what does awareness mean?

In this context the example of ghosts (Chapter 6) is a good example. The one who tries to know themselves by thought identity, or says that they do know themselves, is exactly like someone who says they know the ghosts in the room. Your mind can claim to be aware only when it no longer has a perception of ghosts.

A mind that serves thought identity and has been partitioned into uncountable delusions can never see anything clearly. The illumination and awareness in the true sense is only possible with a "whole mind," not with a fragmented mind. In the partitioned mind, one of the "Is" or the delusions tries to know the rest of the delusions, and this is a useless and deceptive work.

**Q:** *Back to the subject of dreaming, psychologists believe that dreams are necessary and inevitable for humans. What is your opinion?*

**A:** Many of the opinions, laws, and necessities that exist in current societies are necessities for unhealthy people, according to Rumi, these are the "afflicted." Yes, dreams for the one who is identified by thought are a necessity arisen from disease. As long as we live with this phenomenon of thought identity, our mind's correlation with life will be incongruent and incomplete. And the main role of dreaming is in fact to repair and whitewash these partial and conflictive viewpoints.

Therefore we could say that as long as thought identity exists, dreams are a necessary and an inevitable matter. But the whole point is that dreams are like thought polyps within our beings, inauthentic and unnecessary. If this "I" thought did not exist, neither would dreams. A life without thought identity is clear, explicit, and complete. During the day, we would no longer hide anything in the back of our minds so as to dream about it during the night.

Let me say again that once the mind is liberated from thought identity and all of its current noise and babblings, it has a quality of openness and readiness to perceive the unknown mysteries of human existence. With such a quality, in wakefulness as well as in sleep, the mind receives fresh messages that are beyond our present faculties. These messages do not have a dreamlike quality and are different from what we ordinarily know as dreams.

In this context, Rumi has articulated the following verses:

از درون خویش این آوازها
منع کن تا کشف گردد رازها
رنگ ها بینی بجز این رنگ ها
گوهران بینی بجای سنگ ها
گوهر چه! بلکه دریایی شوی
آفتاب چرخ پیمایی شوی

*Contain the bellows of the inner mind,*
*Thereby the soul's secrets you will find.*

*Colors you will see the kind you have never seen,*
*Jewels you will see unlike the stones you have seen.*

*Jewel is naught! For you will be the ocean,*
*The Sun, the track, the orbiting motion.*

**Q:** *How is it possible for the mind to discern when it is in "passive" quality or in "active" quality?*

**A:** I describe this problem in a broader sense, as well as ask a few questions of my own.

*When a question is posed to your mind or there is any movement in your mind, pay attention to your mental quality and see if these three general characteristics have become a part of the movement of your mind or not:*

*First, does the mind use time in its movement? Does it oscillate in time or does it not?*

*Secondly, does the mind use memory to travel into the past? Meaning is the origin of a thought a part of the brain's memory or not?*

*Thirdly, is the movement of the mind a partial movement, or is the mind participating with its entirety?*

For instance, as you sit here, your mind is certainly thinking about something. Now, pay attention to your thoughts to see where they are coming from. Are they arising from memory, or are they not related to memory? If thought is arising from memory, this means it has originated from the "I," and that the answer to the subject will be searched for and found by the "I" as well. Essentially, no matter how far thought strives to move forward, it moves along with the "I."

Now can a question be asked, from yourself or anyone else, in which the mind is free of these three mentioned characteristics? Can you see from this what quality the mind has? Is it possible to put forward a question that does not have one of these three characteristics?

**Q:** *It doesn't seem possible. Without these characteristics no subject or problem comes to mind.*

**A:** This is correct. No problem arises in the mind. But can you say why it does not? The answer is very obvious. If a question or problem does not have one of these characteristics, there is no work for the mind. Any problem that comes to the mind has its roots in memory. The repository of our problems is the memory.

Now, if the mind's relationship to memory is cut off, this means that the mind's relationship to problems is cut off, and when this happens, the mind has the quality of a polished and lucid mirror that reflects everything clearly as it is. *The reason for ignorance and obscuration of the mind is the content of memory.* The veil or obscuration in the mind is the function of the memory itself. Or, more accurately put, the nature of the mind is darkness and ignorance. When this veil or quality of darkness ceases its interference in mind activity, the mind is automatically resting in the truth and therefore it becomes empty of problems.

Try this now and see what change may happen in your mind. Try not to control the memory as it comes to the mind, and just pay attention to whether memory interjects itself into your think-ing. When you do this, you will see that during the entire period of your "attention," the mind is free of all noise and experiences a magnificent change. It is like a cancerous tumor being dis-solved in the human brain, and the brain becomes strangely tran-quil, something that it has never been experienced before. In this experience, all barriers and boundaries within the mind are re-moved and we experience ourselves as infinite expansion. And that is the end of the problem.

# ABOUT THE AUTHOR

The author (right) with translator – Sept 2013 Tehran, Iran

M. J. Mossafa is a contemporary best-selling Persian author. In this book, he offers a pioneering approach to crack the code of human behavior. Mossafa is the author of many books on Sufism and self-realization, including a great work on the essential teachings of Rumi's *Masnavi*. He has authored a total of eight books and published twelve English-to-Persian translations, nine works of J. Krishnamurti, and three of Dr. Karen Horney, the famed psychologist. He has been teaching spirituality and self-realization for more than four decades.

6042814R00141

Printed in Germany
by Amazon Distribution
GmbH, Leipzig